D1557792

ISBN 0-941676-43-9

00043>

7   16598 00043   7

Rice

Traditional Chinese Cooking 傳統篇

作　　　　者	林麗華
翻　譯　顧　問	葛潔輝
出　　版　　者	純青出版社有限公司
	台北市松江路125號5樓
	郵政劃撥12106299
	電話：(02)5074902 . 5084331
著 作 財 產 權 人	財團法人味全文化教育基金會
印　　　　刷	秋雨印刷股份有限公司

Author	Lee Hwa Lin
Translation Consultant	Connie Wolhardt
Publisher	Chin Chin Publishing Co., Ltd.
	5th fl., 125, Sung Chiang Rd, Taipei, Taiwan, R.O.C.
	TEL:(02)5074902 . 5084331
Copyright Holder	Wei-Chuan Cultural-Educational Foundation
Printer	Choice Communications Corp
	Printed in Taiwan R.O.C.
Distributor	Wei-Chuan Publishing
	1455 Monterey Pass Rd, #110
	Monterey Park, CA 91754, U.S.A.
	TEL:(213)2613880 . 2613878
	FAX:(213)2613299

序

中國人是「米的民族」，大江南北的中華兒女依米的特性，精研出各種品嚐「米」的方法；然而，在時代腳步快速變遷下，許多傳統米食的烹調技巧，快被現代化的巨輪輾碎了。

針對這點，我以二年的時間，彙集了一百六十六道「米食食譜」，並且分類為「家常篇」與「傳統篇」兩本。「家常篇」中是以米加上一般材料烹調出膾炙人口的佳餚；而「傳統篇」除了有些較精緻的菜餚外，也包含有古時風味的簡餐及點心，期盼為中國文化傳承奉獻一份心力。

在這本「傳統篇」米食食譜裡，有些為現今都市幾乎快看不到的米食，例如鼎邊銼、鳳片糕、甘薯粥、豬腸糙米粥、倫教糕……等，都是簡單、易學，但是快失傳的美食。

在一般印象中，現代人常受困於「傳統」兩字，總認為「傳統」是老朽、是複雜、甚至艱澀，其實，本書所呈現的「傳統米食」，做法單純，只要材料買得到，可輕而易舉製作一份傳統風情的米食大餐或點心。

西風東漸，在歐美速食瀰漫下，如何給孩子一點老祖宗的美食傳承。可在這本「傳統篇」米食中，深得其中精奧。

Foreword

The Chinese is a race raised on rice. With rice's own distinct characteristics, sons and daughters of Chinese ancestry along the Yangtzu River have created special regional rice dishes over the centuries. In the current rapid pace of changes, many of the traditional recipes are facing extinction under the giant wheels of modernization.

Wei-Chuan Cultural Educational Foundation, within two year's time, gathered one hundred and sixty-six rice recipes. They have been divided into two volumes -- Rice Home Cooking and Rice Traditional Cooking. In the Rice Home Cooking edition, delicious rice dishes are prepared with common materials. In the Rice Traditional Cooking, besides a selection of exquisite rice recipes, also included is a collection of ancient gourmet rice courses and snacks. The Wei-Chuan Foundation`s effort in documenting the Chinese culinary culture is again presented to our customers.

In this edition, Rice Traditional Cooking, many of the recipes in this book are disappering in modern cities. Recipes such as Dia Bean So, Quick Method Dessert, Yam Congee, Brown Rice Congee, Run Jiau Rice Cake are actually simple to learn and easy to make, but are soon to become a lose art.

Generally, modern people have the wrong impression of the word "traditional", which brings to mind a vision of the old and the decadent, complexity, and difficulty. In fact, the traditional recipes presented here are easy. As long as the materials are obtainable, it is a simple delight to whip up a rice gourmet meal or snack.

In this society strongly influenced by western fast food, if may be beneficial to give our children a tough of our ancestral culinary culture.

Lee Hwa Lin

目錄 Contents

粥類 • *Congee*

米漿類 • *Rice puree*

漿糰類 • *Rice Dough*

米粉類 • *Rice Noodles*

熟粉類 • *Roasted Rice*

重量換算表 • *Measurement Equivalents*

1磅 = 454公克 = 16盎士
1盎士 = 28.4公克
1lb.= 454gm (454g.) = 16oz.
1oz. = 28.4gm (28.4g.)

量器說明 • *Table of Measurements*

1杯 = 236c.c. = 1 cup (1C.)
1大匙 = 1湯匙 = 15c.c. = 1 Tablespoon (1T.)
1小匙 = 1茶匙 = 5c.c. = 1 Teaspoon (1t.)

飯的煮法 • *Cooking Methods of Rice*

1 蓬萊米1杯（200公克），洗淨瀝乾再加水1杯，放入電鍋中外鍋加水 ¼ 杯煮至電鍋跳起，再續燜五分鐘即為白飯（約415公克）。

2 圓糯米1杯（200公克），洗淨瀝乾再加水 ⅘ 杯，放入電鍋中外鍋加水 ¼ 杯煮至電鍋跳起，再續燜五分鐘即為糯米飯（約390公克）。

3 長糯米1杯（190公克），洗淨瀝乾再加水 ¾ 杯，放入電鍋中外鍋加水 ¼ 杯煮至電鍋跳起，再續燜五分鐘即為糯米飯（約360公克）。另長糯米洗淨後泡水2小時，再瀝乾水分，入蒸鍋中蒸20分鐘至熟（約330公克）是糯米飯另一做法。

■ 本食譜之白飯是指用蓬萊米所煮成之飯。

1 To cook Japonica Rice (Short Grain Rice): Rinse 1C. (200g. or 7oz.) japonica rice, drain. Add 1C. water and place in a rice cooker, add ¼C. water in the outer pot, then cook until rice cooker shuts off. Continue simmering for 5 minutes extra. Makes 415g. or 14³/₅oz. cooked rice.

2 To cook Short Grain Glutinous Rice: Rinse 1C. (200g. or 7oz.) short grain glutinous rice, drain. Add ⅘C. water and place in a rice cooker, add ¼C. water in the outer pot, and cook until rice cooker shuts off. Continue simmering for 5 minutes extra. Makes 390g. or 13¼oz. cooked glutinous rice.

3 To cook Long Grain Glutinous Rice: Rinse 1C. (190g. or 6²/₃oz.) long grain glutinous rice, drain. Add ¾C. water and place in a rice cooker, add ¼C. water in the outer pot, and cook until rice cooker shuts off. Continue simmering for 5 minutes extra. Makes 360g. or 12 ²/₃oz. cooked glutinous rice. Or: soak long grain glutinous rice in water for 2 hours, drain. Steam for 20 minutes or until cooked (makes 330g. or 11³/₅oz.).

■ All cooked rice recipes in this book use cooked short grain rice, unless otherwise indicated.

飯與水的添加計量表 • *Proportion Chart of Rice and Water*

1 若用電子鍋煮飯，則內鍋水分與電鍋煮法相同，但外鍋不需加水。其水分添加計算如下表。

類別	蓬萊米或在來米			圓糯米		長糯米		
米量（公克）	480	300	240	300	200	400	300	480
添加水量（杯）	2 ²/₅	1 ½	1 ⅕	1 ⅕	⅘	1 ³/₅	1 ⅕	1 ⅘

1 If cooking by eletronic rice cooker, no water is needed for outer pot. Water added in the rice is the same as rice cooker. The proportion of rice and water are as following.

Name	Japonica Rice (Short Grain Rice) Indica Rice (Long Grain Rice)			Short Grain Glutinous Rice		Long Grain Glutinous Rice		
Weight of Rice (g.)	480	300	240	300	200	400	300	480
(oz.)	17	10½	8²/₅	10½	70	14	10½	17
Volume of Water (cups)	2²/₅	1½	1⅕	1⅕	⅘	1³/₅	1⅕	1⁴/₅

特殊材料的製作 · *Preparation Methods of Special Ingredient*

高湯的製作 · *Stock*

1 以豬、牛、雞的肉或骨入沸水中川燙。
2 再將肉或骨頭取出洗淨。
3 以另一鍋水燒開後，再入洗淨的肉或骨頭，並加少許蔥、薑、酒慢火熬出來的湯，謂之高湯。

1 Scald pork, beef, chicken or bones in boiling water.
2 Lift out and rinse.
3 Bring clean water to a boil, add meat or bones together with a little green onion, ginger, and cooking wine. Simmer over low heat until the soup is tasty.

1　2

3

米粉的煮法 · *Rice Noodles*

1 米粉的種類有乾的、濕的、粗的、細的等四種。
2 水煮開，入米粉煮軟後隨即撈起，再入鍋炒或煮均可。
3 米粉亦可直接泡冷水或熱水至軟後撈出再入鍋炒或煮均可。

1 There are four kinds of rice noodles:
　a. dried　b. fresh　c. thin　d. thick
2 Bring water to a boil, add rice noodles to cook until softened. Remove immediately. May be used for frying or in soup.
3 Instead of boiling, rice noodles may also be soaked in cold or warm water until softened. Drain and use for frying or in soup.

1　2

3

鍋粑的製作 · *Crisp Rice Cakes*

1 圓糯米洗淨，以糯米十分之九的水分略為浸泡，入電鍋煮熟後，打鬆吹涼再平舖於烤盤上。
2 將米飯壓緊，入烤箱中，以７０℃烤至米粒全乾即可取出切塊，是為鍋粑。

1 Rinse short grain glutinous rice, soak in water (in proportion of 9/10 to rice) for a while. Cook in rice cooker until done. Break loose, let cool and spread a even layer on a baking sheet.
2 Pack tight the rice layer, and place in a 70°C (158°F) oven until rice is all dried. Cut into serving pieces for crisp rice cakes.

1　2

酒釀的製作 • *Fermented Wine Rice*

- 圓糯米 3 杯洗淨，加水 3 杯煮熟後，打鬆吹涼。
- 酒麴 1．5 公克，壓碎拌入米飯中。
- 米飯裝入玻璃罐（罐子須擦乾），置於陰涼處使其發酵即為酒釀。

- Rinse 3C. short grain glutinous rice, add 3C. water and cook until done. Break loose and let cool.
- Crush 1.5g. fermenting yeast (peka), and mix into the rice.
- Put into a clean jar (must be wiped dry) and leave it at a cool and dark place to ferment.

1   2

3

熟粉的製作 • *Roasted Rice Flour*

熟粉的種類有熟糯米粉及熟在來米粉，其製作方法為米磨成的粉末入鍋小火乾炒 1 0 - 1 5 分鐘至香味出來，且顏色由白色轉為淡黃色即可。

There are two kinds of roasted rice flour, one is roasted glutinous rice flour, the other roasted Indica rice flour. The methods are the same: Ground the rice into fine powder, stir fry in a wok over low heat for 10 - 15 minutes until fragrant. The color should turn into a light yellow.

1

河粉的製作 • *Flat Rice Sheets*

在來米 --------- 2 0 0 公克   太白粉 ------------- 1 ½ 大匙

米洗淨泡水 2 小時後，瀝乾再加 2 杯水入果汁機中打成米漿，續入太白粉拌勻備用。

平盤中塗少許沙拉油，再倒入薄薄一層米漿，入鍋蒸 1 0 分鐘，取出待涼即可。

00g.(7oz.) - Indica rice   1½T. -------- corn starch
ong grain rice)

- Rinse rice and soak in water for 2 hours. Drain and add 2C. water, puree in a blender. Mix well with corn starch.
- Grease a flat pan with a little salad oil, pour in a thin layer of rice puree. Steam for 10 minutes, remove and allow to cool.

1   2

五香蒸肉粉的製作 • *Five-Spice-Flavored Rice Powder*

圓糯米、蓬萊米 -------------
------------- 各１５０公克

1 ⌈五香粉、肉桂粉、花
椒粉 ---------- 各½小匙⌋

1 米洗淨瀝乾，入乾鍋內以小火炒至水乾後，再加 **1** 料一起拌
炒至米呈焦黃色，取出待涼。
2 將炒好的米粒以擀麵棍碾碎即可。

1   2

150g.(5⅓oz.)each -----
short grain glutinous
rice, japonica rice (short
grain rice)

1 ⌈•½t.each five spices
powder, cinnamon
powder, Szechwan
pepper powder⌋

1 Rinse rice and drain. Stir fry in a wok over low
heat until dry. Stir in **1** and fry until rice turns into
a burned yellow color. Remove and let cool.
2 Crush rice with a rolling pin into fine powder.

粿粉糰的製作 • *Rice Flour Dough*

1 圓糯米６００公克洗淨，加水浸泡３小時後，瀝乾水分，分兩次將米加水用果汁機或磨米機製成米漿，裝入
棉布袋中。
2 布袋口紮緊，用重物壓乾或用脫水機脫去水分。
3 脫水到剩約８００公克之粉糰即為粿粉糰。
4 粿粉糰之另一做法為市售糯米粉或在來米粉（兩者亦可稱粿粉）加水揉成之糰。

粿粉糰之米重與粿粉之重量換算	
米重	粿粉重量
６００公克	４８０公克
９００公克	７２０公克

粿粉加水揉成粿粉糰之比例		
粿粉重量	加水量	粿粉糰重量
４８０公克	1⅓杯	８００公克
７２０公克	2杯	１２００公克

1 Rinse 600g. (1⅓lb.) short grain glutinous rice, soak in water for 3 hours, drain. Divide into 2
portions, add water and puree in a blender. Puree both and place into a cloth bag.
2 Tie the bag opening tightly. Press the bag with a heavy weight or drainer to drain off all liquid.
3 Drain until the dough weighs about 800g. (1¾lb.). This is the rice flour dough ready for use.
4 Or: purchase ready-made glutinous rice flour or Indica rice flour (long grain rice flour) in the market
(both are called rice flour), add water and knead into dough.

Weight Equivalent of Rice and Rice Flour for Making Rice Dough	
Weight of Rice	Weight of Rice Flour
600g. or 1⅓lb.	480g. or 17oz.
900g. or 2lb.	720g. or 1½oz.

Proportion of Rice Flour and Water for Making Rice Dough		
Weight of Rice Flour	Volume of Water	Weight of Rice Dough
480g. or 17oz.	1⅓C.	800g. or 1¾lb.
720g. or 1½lb.	2C.	1200g. or 2⅗lb.

材料前處理 • *Preparation of Basic Materials*

蔥段的切法 • *Green Onion Sections*

蔥洗淨。
去頭、尾部分。
切成 3 公分長段。

Wash green onions.
Trim off the tops and roots.
Cut into 3 cm (1⅕") long sections.

1

2

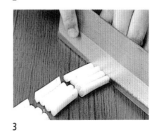
3

香菇的處理 • *Dried Black Mushrooms*

香菇用熱水泡軟再洗淨。
去蒂頭即可。

Soften the mushrooms in warm water, rinse.
Discard the stems.

1

2

腸的清洗方法 • *Intestines*

大腸、小腸均先將腸壁上之肥油剝掉後清洗乾淨。
翻內面,加麵粉、鹽搓洗幾次後,加水沖洗乾淨。
入開水中川燙後,取出再洗淨即可。
本食譜之大腸、小腸生重是指洗淨而未川燙之重,熟重是指
川燙後再煮至熟爛之重,一般大腸之熟重約只有生重之五分
之一,小腸之熟重約只有生重之三分之一。

For both large pork intestines and small pork
intestines,scrape off outer layer of fat and rinse.
Rub flour and salt mixture into inner and outer
intestines a few times, rinse.
Parboil in boiling water, lift out and wash again.
Raw weight in this cook book means washed but
not yet parboiled. Cooked weight means the net
weight after it has been parboiled and then
simmered tender. Generally speaking, large
intestine's cooked weight is only ⅕ of raw weight;
small intestine's cooked weight is only ⅓ of raw
weight.

1

2

3

蝦仁清洗方法 • *Shrimp*

1 蝦用牙籤由背面挑去腸泥（若帶殼，則先去殼）。
2 加太白粉、鹽，輕輕拌洗。
3 用清水洗淨瀝乾，再用布擦乾水分。

1 Devein the shrimp with toothpick (must be shelled first).
2 Clean shrimp by rubbing gently with corn starch and salt.
3 Rinse under water and drain.

1　2

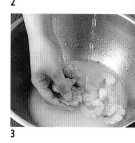

3

筍的處理 • *Bamboo Shoots*

1 新鮮筍中間劃一刀去殼。
2 入水中煮至熟，再取出漂涼即可。若是罐頭筍，有些因製罐關係，會帶有些微酸味，可以先入鍋川燙以去酸味。

1 Cut lengthwise once on the hard outer shell, and peel off all of the outer shell.
2 Boil in water until cooked, drain and let cool.
■ If canned bamboo shoots are used, the taste will be slightly sour due to canning; scald in boiling water to get rid off sour taste before cooking.

1　2

海參的發法 • *Dried Sea Cucumber*

1 乾海參洗淨，泡水一天，隔天換水煮開，煮開後熄火浸泡，待水涼再換水煮開，熄火浸泡，如此一天三次，連續發兩天至軟。
2 由腹部剪開，取出內臟洗淨加水煮開，再發一天即可。
3 若買發好之海參，則剪開肚子取出內臟洗淨即可。

1 Wash the dried sea cucumber, then soak in water for one day. Place sea cucumber into clean water and bring to a boil; turn off the heat and soak until water cools. Change the water again and bring to a boil; turn off the heat and continue soaking until water cools. Repeat the process 3 times a day for 2 days until sea cucumber is softened.
2 Snip open lengthwise and clean out the intestines. Cover with water and bring to a boil. Remove from heat and let it stand for one more day. Then it is ready for cooking.
3 Already soaked sea cucumber can also be bought, then it only needs to be snipped open lengthwise and cleaned out.

1　2

3

花枝的處理・*Squids*

花枝去皮、頸。
去除內臟，並用水洗淨。
花枝肉之內面，每隔０・３公分縱橫切入 ⅓ 深度，使肉身作
交叉片狀。
將片狀花枝切成４公分寬之條狀。
每一條花枝肉再切成４×５公分之片狀。

Discard the neck and peel off the skin.
Discard the inner gut and wash clean.
Score inner surface lengthwise and crosswise
every 0.3 cm (¹⁄₁₀") and ⅓ deep into the flesh.
Cut into 4 cm (1³⁄₅") wide large strips.
Then cut each strip into 4 cm x 5 cm (1³⁄₅" x 2")
serving pieces.

1　2

3　4

5

紅蟳米糕

· *Crab Pilaf*

紅蟳米糕 •*Crab Pilaf*

紅蟳（2隻）------ 6 0 0公克
長糯米 -------------- 4 0 0公克
芋頭(淨重) ---------- 1 0 0公克
里肌肉 ---------------- 7 5公克
胡蘿蔔、叉燒肉 ---各 6 0公克
紅蔥頭 ---------------- 5 0公克
蝦米 ------------------ 3 0公克
蛋 ------------------------ 1個

1┌ 薑片 ----------------- 3片
　└ 酒 ------------------- 1大匙

2┌ 水 ------------------- 1杯
　│ 醬油 --------------- 3大匙
　│ 糖 --------------------½小匙
　└ 五香粉 ------------¼小匙

600g.(1⅓lb.) ---------------------------- crabs (two pieces)
400g.(14oz.) ---------------------- long grain glutinous rice
100g.(3½oz.) ---------------------------- taros (net weight)
75g.(2⅔oz.) --------------------------------------- pork fillet
60g.(2 1/10oz.) each -------------------- carrots, Bar-B-Q pork
50g.(1¾oz.) -------------------------------------- red shallots
30g.(1oz.) ---------------------------- dried baby shrimp
1 --- egg

1┌ •3 slices ginger
　└ •1T.cooking wine

2┌ •1C.water
　│ •3T.soy sauce
　│ •½t.sugar
　└ •¼t.five spices powder

1 米洗淨，泡水 1½ 小時瀝乾，蝦米洗淨，與紅蔥頭均切末備用。
2 紅蟳去除鰓和內臟，洗淨，剁除蟳腳前肢（圖1），再切下蟳螯以刀背拍裂（圖2），蟳身則橫切成四塊（圖3），以 **1** 料醃 1 0分鐘。
3 胡蘿蔔去皮，和芋頭、叉燒肉、里肌肉各切成 1 公分立方的小丁，蛋打散備用。
4 鍋熱入油 1 大匙燒熱，入蛋液炒成蛋花盛起，再入油 3 大匙燒熱，入紅蔥頭、蝦米爆香，續入 **3** 項材料炒香，再入米、**2** 料及蛋拌炒均勻，盛入一大盤中，上置醃好的蟳塊、螯及蟳殼，入鍋大火蒸 1 小時即可。

1 Rinse rice and soak in water for one and half hours, drain. Wash shrimp and mince with shallots.
2 Discard gills and entrails of crabs, wash; cut off forelegs (illus. 1) and claws. With back of knife crack the claws (illus. 2). Cut crab body into quarters (illus. 3), marinate in **1** for 10 minutes.
3 Skin carrots. Cut carrots, taros, Bar-B-Q pork, and pork fillet into 1 cm (⅖") square cubes. Beat the egg.
4 Heat the wok, add 1T. oil and heat; soft stir fry egg, remove. Add 3T. oil and heat, stir fry shallots and shrimp until fragrant. Add step **3** ingredients to fry until fragrant, mix in rice, **2**, and fried egg evenly; remove and place on a large shallow plate. Place crabs, claw, and shell on top. Steam over high heat for one hour and serve.

1

2

3

筒仔米糕

•*Steamed Rice in Bamboo Cups*

筒仔米糕 • *Steamed Rice in Bamboo Cups*

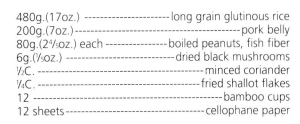

長糯米 ----------- 4 8 0公克	480g.(17oz.) ---------------------long grain glutinous rice
五花肉 ----------- 2 0 0公克	200g.(7oz.)------------------------------------pork belly
熟花生、魚鬆 ------各8 0公克	80g.(2⁴/₅oz.) each ----------------boiled peanuts, fish fiber
香菇 ------------------ 6公克	6g.(¹/₅oz.) ------------------------dried black mushrooms
香菜末 -------------------½杯	½C. -------------------------------------minced coriander
油蔥酥 -------------------¼杯	¼C. -------------------------------------fried shallot flakes
竹筒 ----------------- 1 2個	12 --bamboo cups
玻璃紙 --------------- 1 2張	12 sheets------------------------------------cellophane paper

❶
- 醬油 ----------- 1 大匙
- 酒 ------------- 1 小匙
- 糖、冰糖 --------各½小匙
- 味精 -------------¼小匙
- 胡椒粉 -------------少許

❶
- •1T.soy sauce
- •1t.cooking wine
- •½t.each sugar, crystal sugar
- •dash of pepper

❷
- 高湯 -------------- 1 杯
- 醬油 ----------- 3 大匙
- 酒 -------------½大匙
- 味精、冰糖 ----各¼小匙
- 胡椒粉 -------------少許

❷
- •1C.stock
- •3T.soy sauce
- •½T.cooking wine
- •¼t.crystal sugar
- •dash of pepper

1 長糯米洗淨煮熟，香菇泡軟去蒂切絲備用。

2 五花肉切 1 2塊，入❶料醃約 1 0分鐘，入鍋大火蒸 3 0分鐘，取出備用。

3 鍋熱入油 4 大匙燒熱，入香菇絲爆香，隨入花生及❷料拌勻，再入糯米飯及油蔥酥拌勻，即為油飯，分成 1 2等份備用。

4 取一竹筒，先入 1 份肉（圖 1 ），再入 1 份油飯壓緊（圖 2 ），上蓋 1 張玻璃紙（圖 3 ），共做 1 2份，待水開，入鍋以大火蒸 2 0分鐘，取出倒扣盤中，上面以香菜末及魚鬆裝飾即可。

❶1 食時可沾甜辣醬。

2 米糕上亦可以肉鬆裝飾。

1 Rinse rice and cook until done. Soften mushrooms in warm water, discard stems, and shred.

2 Cut pork into 12 pieces, marinate in ❶ for 10 minutes, steam over high heat for 30 minutes, remove.

3 Heat the wok, add 4T. oil and heat; stir fry shredded mushrooms until fragrant. Add peanuts and ❷ then mix well. Stir in rice and shallot flakes, mix well. Divide into 12 equal portions.

4 Place one piece of pork in a bamboo cup (illus. 1), press in one portion of rice (illus. 2). Seal with one sheet of cellophane paper (illus. 3). Make 12 portions. Bring water to a boil in a large steamer, steam over high heat for 20 minutes. Invert on a platter, decorate with minced coriander and fish fiber. Serve.

❶1 Can be served with Sweet and Spicy Sauce.

2 Pork fiber may be used as garnish.

1

2

3

糯米燒賣 • *Rice Siu Mai*

長糯米 ------------- 300公克		餛飩皮 ------------------ 36張	
紅蔥頭 ------------- 20公克		青豆仁 ------------------ 36顆	

1
- 里肌肉 ------- 100公克
- 蝦米 ------------- 20公克
- 香菇 ------------- 5公克

2
- 醬油 --------------- 4大匙
- 糖 ------------------ 1小匙
- 味精、胡椒粉 --- 各¼小匙

1 糯米煮成糯米飯,肉切絲,香菇泡軟去蒂切絲,紅蔥頭去皮、頭尾並洗淨後切薄片。

2 鍋熱入油2大匙燒熱,入紅蔥頭炒至金黃色,入 **1** 料炒香,續入 **2** 料、糯米飯炒拌均勻即為餡,盛出待涼,分成36等份。

3 每張餛飩皮包入1份餡(圖1),捏成燒賣狀(圖2),上置1顆青豆仁裝飾,再入鍋蒸3分鐘即可。

300g.(10½oz.)-long grain glutinous rice
20g.(⅔oz.)----red shallots

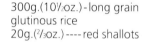
36 ------ wonton wrappers

36 --------------- green peas

1
- •100g.(3½oz.) pork fillet
- •20g.(⅔oz.) dried baby shrimp
- •5g.(⅙oz.) dried black mushrooms

2
- •4T.soy sauce
- •1t.sugar
- •¼t.pepper

1 Steam rice until cooked. Shred pork; soften mushrooms in warm water, discard stems and shred; peel shallots, trim off roots, wash clean and slice thin.

2 Heat the wok, add 2T. oil, stir fry shallots until golden. Add **1** , fry until fragrant; then add **2** and rice, mix well. This is the filling. Spread out on a platter to cool, divide into 36 equal portions.

3 Wrap each filling in the center of a wonton wrapper (illus. 1), squeeze into siu mai shape (illus. 2). Decorate with green peas on top. Steam in a steamer for 3 minutes. Serve hot.

1

2

糯米腸 • *Rice Sausage*

豬大腸 -------------- 600公克		醬油 ---------------- 3 大匙	
長糯米 -------------- 570公克	**1**	酒 ------------------- 1 大匙	
絞肉 ----------------- 100公克		鹽 ------------------- 1 小匙	
蝦米 ------------------- 15公克		味精、胡椒粉 --- 各½小匙	
紅蔥頭片 ------------------ 6 大匙			

1 糯米洗淨，泡水 1 小時後瀝乾備用，大腸洗淨，蝦米亦洗淨瀝乾備用。

2 鍋熱入油 5 大匙燒熱，入紅蔥頭爆香，續入蝦米、絞肉炒至香味出來後，再入糯米及 **1** 料炒拌均勻即為內餡。

3 將內餡塞入大腸中（圖 1 ），約八分滿，且每隔 1 0 公分用棉繩綁緊（圖 2 ）隔斷，全部塞完。

4 將糯米腸放入煮沸的開水中，水須淹過糯米腸煮 3 0 分鐘即可。

600g.(1⅓lb.) --- large pork intestines		100g.(3½oz.) ground pork
570g.(1¼lb.) --- long grain glutinous rice		15g.(½oz.) ----- dried baby shrimp
		6T. ------- red shallot slices

1
- 3T. soy sauce
- 1T. cooking wine
- 1t. salt
- ½t. pepper

1 Wash rice, soak in water for one hour; drain. Wash intestines and dried baby shrimp, drain.

2 Heat the wok, add 5T. oil and heat; stir fry shallots until fragrant. Stir in shrimp and pork, fry until pungent. Add rice and **1**, mix well to create the filling.

3 Stuff the filling into the intestines (illus. 1), about 80% full. Tie tightly with cotton string every 10 cm (4") (illus. 2) to form links.

4 Drop links into boiling water, water should cover the links. Boil for 30 minutes.

1

2

脆皮糯米飯

·*Crispy Rice Balls*

脆皮糯米飯 •*Crispy Rice Balls*

長糯米 ------------- 450公克	450g.(1lb.) ------------------------ long grain glutinous rice

1
- 臘肉、雞胸肉 -------------- ------------ 各150公克
- 蝦米 ------------- 20公克
- 香菇 ------------- 10公克

1
- •150g.(5⅓oz.) each Chinese bacon, chicken breast
- •20g.(⅔oz.) dried baby shrimp
- •10g.(⅓oz.) dried black mushrooms

2
- 水 ------------------ 1杯
- 醬油 ----------------- 2大匙
- 糖 ------------------ 1小匙
- 鹽 ------------------ ½小匙
- 胡椒粉 -------------- ¼小匙

2
- •1C.water
- •2T.soy sauce
- •1t.sugar
- •½t.salt
- •¼t.pepper

3
- 低筋麵粉 ------------- 1杯
- 水 ----------------- ¾杯
- 豬油 ---------------- 2大匙
- 泡打粉、太白粉各1小匙

3
- •1C.low gluten flour
- •¾C.water
- •2T.lard
- •1t.each baking powder, corn starch

1 糯米洗淨泡水2小時，瀝乾水分，入鍋蒸熟備用。
2 蝦米、香菇泡軟洗淨切細丁，臘肉入鍋川燙取出切細丁，雞胸肉亦切細丁。
3 鍋熱入油4大匙燒熱，入**1**料爆香，再入**2**料拌炒均勻，隨即拌入蒸熟糯米飯拌勻起鍋待涼，分成20等份，每份約40公克，並捏成圓形（圖1）。
4 將**3**料調勻成糊狀備用。
5 鍋熱入油8杯燒至九分熱（200℃），把做好糯米球沾上**3**料（圖2），入油鍋炸至金黃色即可。

1 Rinse rice and soak in water for 2 hours, drain. Steam until cooked.
2 Wash shrimp and mushrooms, soften in warm water, and finely dice. Parboil Chinese bacon in boiling water, remove, and finely dice. Dice chicken breast.
3 Heat the wok, add 4T. oil and heat; stir fry **1** until fragrant, mix evenly with **2**. Then mix in cooked rice well, cool. Divide into 20 equal portions, about 40g. (1⅖oz.) each. Pack each portion into a ball by hand (illus. 1).
4 Mix **3** into thin batter.
5 Heat the wok, add 8C. oil and heat to 200°C (392°F), dip rice ball into **3** (illus. 2). Deep fry until golden.

1

2

肉粽

• *Pork Rice Dumplings in Bamboo Leaves*

肉粽 • *Pork Rice Dumplings in Bamboo Leaves*

長糯米 ------------- 600公克	600g.(1⅓lb.) ---------------------- long grain glutinous rice
夾心肉 ------------- 200公克	200g.(7oz.) --------------------------------- pork shoulder
蝦米 --------------- 35公克	35g.(1¼oz.) -------------------------------- dried baby shrimp
香菇 --------------- 6公克	6g.(⅕oz.) ------------------------------- dried black mushrooms
粽葉 --------------- 24張	24 ----------------------------------- broad bamboo leaves
粽繩 --------------- 12條	12 -- bamboo strings
栗子 --------------- 12個	12 --- chestnuts
滷蛋 --------------- 3個	3 ------------------------------------ soy sauce braised eggs
油蔥酥 ------------- 2大匙	2T. -------------------------------------- fried shallot flakes
蒜末 --------------- 1大匙	1T. -- minced garlic

1
- 醬油 ------------- 3大匙
- 酒 --------------- ½小匙
- 味精、糖、胡椒粉 -------- 各¼小匙

1
- •3T.soy sauce
- •½t.cooking wine
- •¼t.each sugar, pepper

2
- 醬油 ------------- 2大匙
- 鹽 --------------- ¾小匙
- 味精、胡椒粉 --- 各¼小匙

2
- •2T.soy sauce
- •¾t.salt
- •¼t.pepper

1 糯米洗淨泡水約1小時，瀝乾水分，粽葉、粽繩洗淨備用。

2 肉切為12塊，香菇泡軟去蒂亦切12塊。另將栗子洗淨，加水蓋過栗子，蒸熟備用。

3 鍋熱入油1大匙燒熱，炒香蒜末，入 **1** 料及肉翻炒數次，加水1杯，連同滷蛋、栗子、香菇，改小火煮至汁收乾，滷蛋1切為4。

4 鍋熱入油4大匙燒熱，將蝦米炒香，再入油蔥酥、糯米及 **2** 料拌炒，並不時加水炒至米半熟。

5 2張粽葉頭尾重疊折成三角形（圖1），包入糯米、肉、香菇、栗子、滷蛋（圖2），再放入少許糯米，包成粽子狀（圖3），以粽繩繫好（圖4），入鍋再蒸1小時即可。

1 Wash rice, soak in water for 1 hour; drain. Wash bamboo leaves and strings

2 Cut pork into 12 equal pieces. Soften mushrooms in warm water, discard stems and cut into 12 equal pieces. Wash chestnuts, cover with water and steam until cooked.

3 Heat the wok, add 1T. oil and heat, stir fry garlic until fragrant; add **1** and pork, stir fry a while. Add 1C. water, eggs, chestnuts, and mushrooms, simmer over low heat until water dried out. Cut each egg into quarters.

4 Heat the wok, add 4T. oil and heat, stir fry shrimp until fragrant. Add shallot flakes, rice, and **2**, stir fry well and add a little water whenever needed until rice is half cooked.

5 With 2 leaves, fold into a cone (illus. 1). Wrap in rice, pork, mushrooms, chestnuts, and eggs (illus. 2); cover with a little rice. Fold into a dumpling (illus. 3), tie with string (illus. 4). Steam for 1 hour and serve.

1

2

3

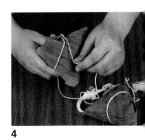
4

紅豆鹼粽 • *Red Bean Soda Dumplings*

圓糯米 ------------- ３００公克	粽繩 ----------------------- ２２條
紅豆 ----------------- １００公克	鹼粉 ----------------------- ２小匙
粽葉 ----------------------- ４４張	

1 紅豆洗淨泡水３０分鐘，瀝乾，粽葉泡軟與粽繩均洗淨備用。
2 糯米洗淨泡水２小時，瀝乾，與紅豆、鹼粉拌勻，分成２２等份。
3 每２張粽葉頭尾重疊折成三角形，放入１份紅豆糯米，包成粽子狀（包時須留有空隙，不要裝滿），入沸水中煮１小時即可。

300g.(10½oz.) ------- short grain glutinous rice	44 - broad bamboo leaves
100g.(3½oz.) --- red beans	22 --------- bamboo strings
	2t. ------------ baking soda

1 Wash red beans and soak in water for 30 minutes, drain. Wash bamboo leaves and strings.
2 Rinse rice and soak in water for 2 hours, drain. Mix well with red beans and soda, divide into 22 equal portions.
3 Fold 2 bamboo leaves into a cone, fill in one portion of fillings. Wrap into dumpling (wrap loosely, do not fill up the filling completely). Boil in boiling water for 1 hour.

鹼粽 • *Soda Dumplings*

圓糯米 ------------- ３００公克	粽繩 ----------------------- ２０條
粽葉 ----------------------- ４０張	鹼粉 ----------------------- ２小匙

1 米洗淨泡水２小時，瀝乾水分，加鹼粉拌勻，分成２０等份。
2 粽葉洗淨，每２張粽葉頭尾重疊折成三角形，裝入１份糯米，包成粽子狀（包時須留有空隙，不要裝滿），以粽繩繫好。
3 鍋中加水煮沸入粽子（水須淹過粽子），煮約２小時至熟取出，待冷卻即可，食時可沾糖漿或蜂蜜。

300g.(10½oz.) ------- short grain glutinous rice	20 --------- bamboo strings
40 - broad bamboo leaves	2t. ------------ baking soda

1 Rinse rice and soak in water for 2 hours, drain. Mix well with soda, divide into 20 equal portions.
2 Wash bamboo leaves. Fold 2 leaves into a cone, fill in one portion of rice fillings. Wrap into dumpling (wrap loosely, do not fill up completely). Tie with bamboo strings.
3 Bring a large pot of water to boil, add dumplings (water must cover dumplings). Boil for 2 hours, remove. When cooled, serve with syrup or honey.

鍋粑蝦仁 • *Sizzling Rice Cake with Shrimp*

蝦仁 ----------------- 225公克	蔥段 ------------------------- 4 段
鍋粑 ----------------- 120公克	薑片 ------------------------- 3 片
青豆仁 -------------- 50公克	麻油 ------------------------- 1 大匙

1
- 蛋白 ---------------- ½個
- 太白粉 -------------- 2 小匙
- 鹽 ------------------ ¼小匙

2
- 水或高湯 ------------- 2 杯
- 番茄醬 -------------- 3 大匙
- 糖 ------------------ 1 大匙
- 醬油 ----------------- ½大匙
- 鹽 ------------------ ¼小匙

3 太白粉、水 ------- 各2大匙

1 蝦仁洗淨瀝乾水分，入 **1** 料拌醃20分鐘，鍋粑切3公分之塊狀。

2 鍋熱入油6杯燒至七分熱（160℃），入鍋粑炸至金黃色，撈起置於大盤內備用。

3 蝦仁入油鍋以中火（約120℃）泡熟撈出，鍋內留油3大匙燒熱，隨即入蔥、薑爆香，再入 **2** 料及青豆仁，待滾後放入蝦仁，並以 **3** 料苟芡，灑上麻油淋於鍋粑上即可。

225g.(8oz.) -------- shelled shrimp	50g.(1¾oz.) -- green peas
120g.(4⅓oz.) ---- crisp rice cakes	4 sections ---- green onion
	3 slices -------------- ginger
	1T. -------------- sesame oil

1
- ½ egg white
- 2t.corn starch
- ¼t.salt

2
- 2C.stock or water
- 3T.ketchup
- 1T.sugar
- ½T.soy sauce
- ¼t.salt

3
- 2T.each corn starch, water

1 Wash and dry shrimp; marinate with **1** for 20 minutes. Cut rice cakes into 3 cm (1⅕") squares.

2 Heat the wok, add 6C. oil; heat to 160°C (320°F). Deep fry rice cakes until golden. Place on a large platter.

3 Dip shrimp in oil (120°C/248°F) until cooked and remove. Keep 3T. oil in the wok. Stir fry green onion and ginger until fragrant; add **2** and green peas. After boiling, add shrimp; thicken with **3**. Sprinkle on sesame oil and pour over rice cakes; serve immediately.

豆沙粽 • *Sweet Rice Dumplings in Bamboo Leaves*

圓糯米 --------------- 600公克	粽葉 --------------------- 16張	
豆沙 ----------------- 200公克	粽繩 --------------------- 8條	

1 米洗淨泡水3小時瀝乾水分，分成8等份；粽葉、粽繩洗淨備用。

2 豆沙餡分成8等份，搓成長條形，備用。

3 粽葉2張頭尾重疊折成長三角形（圖1），先放入½份糯米，再放入豆沙餡（圖2），上面再覆上½份糯米包成長條狀，以粽繩繫好（圖3）。

4 鍋中加水煮沸入粽子（水須淹過粽子），煮2～3小時即成。

600g.(1⅓lb.) -- short grain glutinous rice
200g.(7oz.) ----- sweet red bean paste

16 - broad bamboo leaves
8 ---------- bamboo strings

1 Wash rice and soak in water for 3 hours, drain; divide into 8 equal portions. Wash bamboo leaves and strings.

2 Divide red bean paste into 8 equal portions, shape into long strips.

3 Place 2 bamboo leaves in double layer, fold one half into long triangle (illus. 1). Place half portion of rice in, add sweet bean paste in the center (illus. 2); top with the other half of rice. Fold over the other half of the leaves into a oblong shape. Tie with string (illus. 3).

4 Bring a large pot of water to boil, drop in the dumplings (water must cover the dumplings). Boil for 2 - 3 hours.

1

2

3

潮州肉粽 • *Chao Chow Rice Dumplings in Bamboo Leaves*

長糯米、五花肉 各600公克	粽葉 ----------------- 20張	600g.(1⅓lb.) each ---long grain glutinous rice, pork belly	6g.(⅕oz.) ------dried black mushrooms
紅蔥頭、蝦米 ------各50公克	粽繩 ----------------- 10條		20 -broad bamboo leaves
香菇 ----------------- 6公克	醬油 ----------------- 2大匙	50g.(1¾oz.) each -----red shallots,dried baby shrimp	20 ---------bamboo strings
			2T. ---------------soy sauce

1 鹽、味精 ----------- 各¼小匙

2
- 醬油 ----------- 1½大匙
- 酒 ----------------- 1大匙
- 鹽 ----------------- 1小匙
- 味精 ----------------- ¼小匙

1 •¼t.salt

2
- •1½T.soy sauce
- •1T.cooking wine
- •1t.salt

1 糯米洗淨泡水2小時後瀝乾,加**1**料拌勻,分成10份。
2 五花肉切成10塊,入**2**料醃30分鐘。
3 紅蔥頭洗淨去皮切片,蝦米、香菇泡軟,香菇去蒂切絲。
4 鍋熱入油2大匙燒熱,入紅蔥頭爆香至金黃色,再入蝦米、香菇炒香,再加2大匙醬油及五花肉拌炒均勻,盛起分成10等份。
5 粽葉粽繩洗淨,取2張粽葉,頭尾重疊折成長三角形,先放入½份糯米,上置1份餡料,再覆上½份糯米,包成長條狀以粽繩繫好。
6 鍋中加水煮沸入粽子(水須淹過粽子),煮2小時即可。

1 Rinse rice and soak in water for 2 hours, drain. Mix with **1** well, and divide into 10 equal portions.
2 Cut pork belly into 10 equal pieces, marinate with **2** for 30 minutes.
3 Wash shallots, peel off skin, and slice. Soften shrimp and mushrooms in warm water. Discard stems from mushrooms and slice.
4 Heat the wok, add 2T. oil and heat; stir fry shallots until golden. Stir in shrimp and mushrooms to fry until fragrant. Add 2T. soy sauce and pork, fry, mix evenly, remove and divide into 10 equal portions.
5 Wash bamboo leaves and strings. Double fold two leaves into a long triangle, place half portion of rice in, and a portion of pork filling in the center, cover with other half of rice. Wrap into a long bundle. Tie with strings tightly.
6 Bring a large pot of water to boil, drop in dumplings (water must cover dumplings). Boil for 2 hours.

荷葉飯 • *Rice in Lotus Wrapper*

長糯米 ------------- ３００公克	蝦米 --------------------- １０公克
瘦肉 ---------------- １５０公克	香菇 ----------------------- ５公克
廣式香腸 ------------ ４０公克	荷葉 ------------------------- １張
紅蔥頭 ------------- ２０公克	

1
- 水 --------------------- １½杯
- 醬油 ------------------ ２大匙
- 糖、麻油 -------- 各１小匙
- 味精 ------------------½小匙
- 鹽、五香粉 ------ 各¼小匙

1 糯米洗淨泡水２小時，瀝乾水分；香菇泡軟去蒂，與廣式香腸、瘦肉均切丁；蝦米泡水，瀝乾水分；紅蔥頭切片；荷葉洗淨（圖１）燙過開水（圖２）備用。

2 鍋熱入油１大匙燒熱，入紅蔥頭炒至金黃色撈起，續入瘦肉、蝦米、香菇爆香後，入糯米及 **1** 料，以小火拌炒２～３分鐘，再入紅蔥頭及廣式香腸拌匀，以荷葉包好後，入鍋大火蒸３０分鐘即可。

300g.(10½oz.) - long grain
glutinous rice
150g.(5⅓oz.) --- lean pork
40g.(1²/₅oz.) --- Cantonese
sausage
20g.(²/₃oz.) ---- red shallots

10g.(⅓oz.) ----- dried baby
shrimp
5g.(⅙oz.) ------ dried black
mushrooms
1 sheet ----------- lotus leaf

1
- 1½C.water
- 2T.soy sauce
- 1t.each sugar, sesame oil
- ¼t.each salt, five spices powder

1 Wash rice, cover with water and soak for 2 hours; drain. Soften mushrooms in warm water and discard stems. Dice sausage, pork, and mushrooms. Soften shrimp in water and drain. Slice shallots. Wash Lotus leaf (illus. 1), scald in boiling water and remove (illus. 2).

2 Heat the wok, add 1T. oil; stir fry shallots until golden then remove. Add pork, shrimp, and mushrooms, stir fry until fragrant. Then add rice and **1**, stir fry over low heat for 2 - 3 minutes. Put shallots and sausage back in and mix well. Wrap the filling in lotus leaf, steam over high heat for 30 minutes. Serve.

1

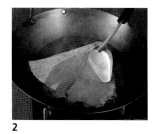

2

香味飯糰 • *Home Style Rice Rolls*

白飯 ----------------- 4 8 0公克	紅蔥頭末 ----------------- 6大匙	480g.(17oz.) - cooked rice	9g.(⅓oz.) ------ dried black mushrooms
里肌肉 ----------------- 7 5公克	熟胡蘿蔔末 -------------- 2大匙	75g.(2⅔oz.) ---- pork fillet	6T. ---- minced red shallot
蝦米 ----------------- 3 0公克	苔菜 --------------------- 1 ½大匙	30g.(1oz.) ----- dried baby shrimp	2T. -- minced boiled carrot
香菇 ----------------- 9公克			1½T. ------- green seaweed

❶
- 醬油 ----------------- 1 大匙
- 酒 --------------------- 2 小匙
- 糖 --------------------- ¾小匙
- 胡椒粉 -------------- ⅛小匙

❶
- •1T.soy sauce
- •2t.cooking wine
- •¾t.sugar
- •⅛t.pepper

1 蝦米、香菇泡軟洗淨，瀝乾水分，與里肌肉均切小丁備用。

2 鍋熱入油３大匙燒熱，入紅蔥頭炒至金黃色，續入蝦米、香菇炒香，最後入里肌肉及 ❶ 料炒熟即為內餡，與白飯均分成６等份備用。

3 取１份白飯鋪在塑膠袋上，上置１份內餡（圖１），包起捏緊成圓形（圖２），即為飯糰，外表再沾上胡蘿蔔或苔菜，依序作完即可。

1 Soften mushrooms and shrimp in warm water, rinse clean, and drain. Dice both and pork fillet into small cubes.

2 Heat the wok, add 3T. oil and heat; stir fry shallot until golden. Add shrimp and mushrooms to fry until fragrant. Stir in pork and ❶, fry until cooked. This is the filling. Divide filling and rice into 6 equal portions.

3 Spread one portion of rice on a plastic sheet, place one portion of filling in the center (illus. 1). Pack tightly into a ball by hand (illus. 2). Dust with minced carrot or green seaweed. Makes 6.

1

2

肉鬆飯糰 · *Rice Balls with Pork Fiber*

白飯	480公克	紫菜	1張
肉鬆	90公克	熟白芝麻	2大匙
蘿蔔乾	60公克	糖	3/8小匙

1 蘿蔔乾洗淨切碎，鍋熱入油1大匙燒熱，入蘿蔔乾炒熟，再入糖拌炒均勻即為內餡，與白飯、肉鬆均分成6等份，另紫菜剪成約0．3公分之條狀備用。

2 取1份白飯舖在塑膠袋上，上置1份內餡與肉鬆，包起捏緊成三角形，外表沾上紫菜條或白芝麻，依序作完即可。

480g.(17oz.) - cooked rice
90g.(3⅕oz.) ---- pork fiber
60g.(2¹/₁₀oz.) - dried turnip
1 sheet ----------- seaweed

2T. --------- roasted white sesame seeds
³/₈t. --------------------- sugar

1 Wash dried turnip and finely chop. Heat the wok, add 1T. oil and heat; stir fry turnip until cooked. Add sugar and mix well, to create the filling. Divide filling, rice, and pork fiber into 6 equal portions. Snip seaweed into 0.3 cm (1⅕") strips.

2 Spread out one portion of rice on a plastic sheet. Place a portion of filling and pork fiber into the center, pack tightly into a ball by hand. Dust on seaweed or white sesame seeds. Makes 6.

鮪魚飯糰 · *Rice Balls with Tuna Fish*

白飯	480公克	**1** 沙拉醬	75公克
罐頭鮪魚	150公克	黑胡椒粉、鹽、白醋	
洋蔥	75公克		各3/8小匙
熟蛋黃	2個		
香鬆	1½大匙		

1 鮪魚搗碎，洋蔥切末，加 **1** 料拌勻為內餡，與白飯均分成6等份。

2 取1份白飯舖在塑膠袋上，上置1份內餡，包起捏緊成方形，外表沾上香鬆或蛋黃末，依序作完即可。

480g.(17oz.) - cooked rice
150g.(5⅓oz.) ------ canned tuna in spring water
75g.(2²/₃oz.) -------- onion
2 -- hard-boiled egg yolks
1½T. -------- seaweed and sesame seasoning

1 •75g.(2²/₃oz.) mayonnaise
•³/₈t.each black pepper, salt, white vinegar

1 Crush tuna into small pieces and mince onion. Mix well with **1** for the filling. Divide both filling and rice into 6 equal portions.

2 Spread out one portion of rice on a plastic sheet, place one filling in the center. Pack tightly into a square by hand, dust on crushed egg yolks or seaweed and sesame seasoning. Makes 6.

鴨肉米糕 • *Duck Pilaf*

鴨肉(去骨) --------- ６００公克	酒 ----------------------------- 1 杯
長糯米 ------------- ４００公克	黑麻油 --------------------- 3 大匙
薑片 ----------------------- 1 2 片	

1 鴨肉切４×４公分塊狀，糯米洗淨備用。
2 鍋熱入黑麻油燒熱，入薑片爆炒至金黃色，續入鴨肉炒至肉變色，再入糯米及水½杯炒至水分收乾，盛入電鍋內鍋中，加酒１杯、水½杯，外鍋加水３杯煮至電鍋跳起，續燜１０分鐘即可。

600g.(1⅓lb.)duck (boned)	12 slices ------------- ginger
400g.(14oz.) --- long grain glutinous rice	1C. ---------- cooking wine
	3T. ------- black sesame oil

1 Cut duck into 4 cm x 4 cm (1³/₅" x 1³/₅") serving pieces. Wash rice.
2 Heat the wok, add sesame oil and heat; stir fry ginger until golden. Stir in duck and fry until color changes. Add rice and ½C. water, stir fry until liquid is reduced. Replace in the inner pot of a rice cooker, mix in 1C. wine and ½C. water; add 3C. water into the outer pot. Steam until rice cooker shuts off, keep pilaf in the cooker for 10 minutes further. Serve.

黑珍珠塔 • *Black Pearl Tart*

黑糯米 -------------- 1 ００公克	豬油 ----------------------- 1 大匙
長糯米 ----------------- 4 ０公克	塔模 ----------------------- 6 個
細糖 ----------------------------¼杯	

1 鋁箔紙墊入塔模中，修除多餘部份備用。
2 黑糯米、長糯米洗淨後，加水浸泡４小時瀝乾水分，入電鍋內鍋中加水¾杯，外鍋加水１杯，煮至電鍋跳起後，續燜１０分鐘，加豬油、細砂糖拌勻，盛入塔模內整型後，再蒸１０分鐘即可。
■ 黑珍珠塔上可飾以櫻桃、蜜糖蓮子或青豆仁以增加美觀。

100g.(3½oz.) --------- black glutinous rice	¼C. -------------------- sugar
40g.(1²/₅oz.) --- long grain glutinous rice	1T. ----------------------- lard
	6 ----------------- tart molds

1 Line tart molds with foil paper, trim off excess foil.
2 Wash black glutinous rice and long grain glutinous rice; soak in water for 4 hours and drain. Place in the inner pot of a rice cooker, add ¾C. water. Pour 1C. water into outer pot and steam until rice cooker shuts off, keep rice in the cooker 10 minutes longer. Mix lard and sugar in evenly, press into molds and steam another 10 minutes. Serve.
■ Cherries, candied lotus seeds, or green peas may be used to decorate the top of the tart.

二人份　**serve 2**

揚州炒飯 • *Fried Rice a la Yang Chow*

白飯 ------------------ ６００公克
熟毛豆仁 -------------- ５０公克
叉燒肉 ---------------- ４０公克
雞胸肉、海參、花枝、蝦仁、
熟洋菇、熟筍 ------ 各３０公克

中式火腿 -------------- ２０公克
雞心、雞胗 ------------ 各１個
蔥末 ------------------- ２大匙

1⌈ 醬油 ---------------- １小匙
　 鹽、黑胡椒粉 --- 各¼小匙

2 蛋白、太白粉、油 - 各少許

1 雞心、雞胗、洋菇、筍、海參均切丁，花枝切花再切片，再依序入開水中燙熟，中式火腿切末，叉燒肉切丁備用。
2 雞胸肉切丁入 **2** 料拌醃，蝦仁切丁入少許蛋白拌醃。
3 鍋熱入油 ½ 杯燒熱，先入雞胸肉過油盛起，再入蝦仁過油盛起。
4 鍋熱入油 ３大匙燒熱，先入蔥末、叉燒肉、中式火腿爆香，續入海參、花枝、雞心、雞胗、洋菇、筍拌炒，隨入白飯及 **1** 料炒勻，最後加上雞胸肉、蝦仁、毛豆仁拌炒均勻即可。

600g.(1⅓lb.) - cooked rice
50g.(1¾oz.) - boiled fresh soy beans
40g.(1²/₅oz.) Bar-B-Q pork
1 each ----- chicken heart, chicken gizzard
2T. -- minced green onion

30g.(1oz.) each -- chicken breast, sea cucumber, squids, shelled shrimp, cooked or canned button mushrooms, cooked or canned bamboo shoots
20g.(²/₃oz.) -- Chinese ham

1⌈ •1t.soy sauce
　 •¼t.each salt, black pepper

2⌈ •dash of each: egg white, corn starch, oil

1 Dice chicken heart, chicken gizzard, mushrooms, bamboo, and sea cucumber. Score diamond shaped slits on the surface of squids and slice. Parboil all above ingredients in boiling water. Mince Chinese ham. Dice Bar-B-Q pork.
2 Dice chicken breast and marinate in **2**. Dice shrimp and mix with a dash of egg white.
3 Heat the wok, add ½C. oil and heat; fry chicken breast in hot oil and remove, then fry shrimp and remove.
4 Heat the wok, add 3T. oil and heat; stir fry green onion, Bar-B-Q pork, and ham until fragrant. Add sea cucumber, squids, chicken heart, gizzard, mushrooms, and bamboo to fry and mix evenly. Stir in rice and **1**, mix well. Then add chicken breast, shrimp, and fresh soy beans, mix well and heat thoroughly. Serve.

廣東炒飯 • *Cantonese Fried Rice*

白飯 ----------------- 600公克	蝦仁 --------------------- 35公克	600g.(1⅓lb.) - cooked rice	6g.(⅕oz.) ------ dried black
叉燒肉 ---------------- 80公克	香菇 ----------------------- 6公克	80g.(2⅘oz.) Bar-B-Q pork	mushrooms
熟青豆仁 ------------- 60公克	蛋 --------------------------- 1個	60g.(2¹⁄₁₀oz.) --------- boiled	1 ------------------------- egg
廣式香腸 ------------- 45公克	蔥白末、蔥綠末 ------ 各2大匙	green peas	2T.each ---- minced green
		45g.(1³⁄₅oz.) --- Cantonese	onion(green part), minced
		sausage	green onion (white part)
		35g.(1¼oz.)shelled shrimp	

1 蛋白、鹽 ------------ 各少許   　**2** ⎡ 鹽 ---------------------- ½小匙
　　　　　　　　　　　　　　　　　⎣ 味精、胡椒粉 --- 各¼小匙

1 ⎡ •dash of each: egg　　**2** ⎡ •½t.salt
　　⎣ white, salt　　　　　　　　⎣ •¼t.pepper

1 蝦仁洗淨切丁，以**1**料醃10分鐘，鍋熱入油½杯燒熱，入蝦仁
　　過油，隨即撈出備用。
2 香菇泡軟去蒂，與叉燒肉、廣式香腸均切小丁，蛋打散備用。
3 鍋熱入油1大匙燒熱，入蛋液炒成蛋花盛起，續入2大匙油燒
　　熱，入蔥白、香菇、叉燒肉、廣式香腸炒香，再入白飯、青豆
　　仁、蝦仁、蛋及**2**料炒勻盛出，灑上蔥綠末即可。

1 Wash shrimp and dice, marinate in **1** for 10 minutes. Heat the wok, add ½C. oil and heat; place shrimp in hot oil, lift out immediately.
2 Soften black mushrooms in warm water, discard the stems. Dice mushrooms, Bar-B-Q pork, and sausage into small cubes. Beat egg.
3 Heat the wok, add 1T. oil and heat; stir fry egg and remove. Add 2T. oil and heat, stir fry the white part of green onion, mushrooms, pork, and sausage until fragrant. Add rice, green peas, shrimp, egg, and **2**, stir fry evenly. Remove, sprinkle on the green part of green onion and serve.

鹹魚雞粒炒飯 • *Fried Rice with Salted Fish*

白飯 ----------------- ６００公克	香菇 ---------------------- ６公克
鹹魚 ----------------- １２０公克	蛋 ------------------------ ２個
雞胸肉 -------------- １００公克	蔥末 --------------------- ６大匙
熟青豆仁 ------------- ６０公克	

１⎡ 鹽 -------------------- ½小匙
　⎣ 味精、胡椒粉 --- 各¼小匙

1 鹹魚去骨，以油３大匙煎熟後，搗碎備用；香菇泡軟切丁。
2 雞胸肉切小丁並加少許蛋白拌醃，其餘蛋打散。
3 鍋熱入油１大匙燒熱，將蛋液炒成蛋花盛起，再加油２大匙燒熱，入蔥末及香菇丁炒香後，續入雞肉炒熟，再入白飯及 **１** 料拌炒均勻，最後拌入鹹魚、蛋花及青豆仁即可。

600g.(1⅓lb.) - cooked rice	6g.(⅕oz.) ------ dried black mushrooms
120g.(4¼oz.) -- salted fish	
100g.(3½oz.) ----- chicken breast	2 ----------------------- eggs
60g.(2¹/₁₀oz.) --------- boiled green peas	6T. -- minced green onion

1⎡ • ½t.salt
　⎣ • ¼t.pepper

1 Debone the fish, saute in 3T. oil until cooked; crush to fine pieces. Soften mushrooms in warm water, discard stems, and dice.
2 Dice chicken breast and marinate with a little egg white. Beat the rest of the eggs.
3 Heat the wok, add 1T. oil, stir fry eggs quickly and remove. Add 2T. oil and heat, stir fry green onion and mushrooms until fragrant; add chicken, stir fry until cooked. Stir in rice and **1**, mix well. Then add salted fish, eggs, and green peas. Mix and cook thoroughly.

豆豉雞球飯 • *Chicken Rice with Black Bean Sauce*

白飯 ------------- 1000公克	豆豉 --------------------- 20公克	1000g.(2⅕lb.) cooked rice	20g.(⅔oz.) ----- fermented
雞肉 ----------------- 150公克	蒜末 ---------------------- 1大匙	150g.(5⅓oz.) ------ chicken	black soy beans
		breast	1T. ----------- minced garlic

1 ┌ 蛋白 -------------------- ½個
　 │ 太白粉、酒 ----- 各2小匙
　 └ 鹽 --------------------- ¼小匙

3 ┌ 水 ------------------------ 4杯
　 │ 醬油 ----------------- 2大匙
　 │ 麻油 ----------------- 2小匙
　 │ 鹽、糖、酒 ----- 各1小匙
　 └ 味精、胡椒粉 --- 各½小匙

1 ┌ •½ egg white
　 │ •2t.each corn starch,
　 │ 　cooking wine
　 └ •¼t.salt

3 ┌ •4C.water
　 │ •2T.soy sauce
　 │ •2t.sesame oil
　 │ •1t.each salt, sugar,
　 │ 　cooking wine
　 └ •½t.pepper

2 ┌ 青椒 ----------- 150公克
　 │ 洋菇 ----------- 140公克
　 │ 胡蘿蔔 ------- 120公克
　 └ 香菇 ----------------- 8公克

4 ┌ 太白粉、水 ------- 各2大匙

2 ┌ •150g.(5⅓oz.) green
　 │ 　pepper
　 │ •140g.(5oz.) button
　 │ 　mushrooms
　 │ •120g.(4¼oz.) carrots
　 │ •8g.(¼oz.) dried black
　 └ 　mushrooms

4 ┌ •2T.each corn starch,
　 └ 　water

1 雞肉用刀背拍鬆，切塊，入 **1** 料拌醃數分鐘。
2 豆豉剁碎，**2** 料洗淨均切片備用。
3 鍋熱入油1杯燒熱，入 **2** 料過油盛起，再入雞肉泡熟撈起，鍋內留油2大匙炒香豆豉及蒜末，續入 **3** 料煮開，再入雞肉及 **2** 料，並以 **4** 料芶芡，淋在白飯上即成。

1 Tenderize chicken with the back of knife, cut into serving pieces; marinate in **1** for a few minutes.
2 Finely chop fermented black soy beans. Wash **2** and slice.
3 Heat the wok, add 1C. oil and heat, place **2** in hot oil and drain. Then fry chicken in hot oil until cooked, drain. Keep 2T. oil in the wok, stir fry fermented black soy beans and garlic until fragrant; add **3** and bring to a boil. Add chicken and **2** ; thicken with **4**. Pour over rice and serve.

豉汁排骨飯 • *Pork Ribs Rice with Black Bean Sauce*

白飯 ------------- 1000公克	薑末 ---------------------- 2大匙	
小排骨 -------------- 300公克	蒜末、豆豉（濕）--- 各1大匙	
蔥末 ----------------------- 6大匙	紅辣椒 --------------------- 1條	

1
┌ 太白粉 ------------- 2大匙
│ 酒 ---------------------- 1小匙
└ 鹽、醬油 --------- 各¼小匙

2
┌ 水 ---------------------- 1杯
│ 醬油 ---------------- 3大匙
│ 糖 ---------------------- 2小匙
│ 酒 ---------------------- 1小匙
└ 胡椒粉、味精 --- 各⅛小匙

1 小排骨入 **1** 料拌醃，紅辣椒去籽切細末。
2 鍋熱入油2杯燒熱，入排骨炸至金黃色撈起。
3 鍋內留油1大匙燒熱，入蒜、薑、辣椒、豆豉及3大匙蔥末炒香，再入 **2** 料煮開，淋於排骨上，入鍋大火蒸50分鐘，取出淋於白飯上，再灑上剩餘的蔥末即可。
■ 食用時，可再搭配蔬菜，以均衡營養。

1000g.(2⅕lb.) cooked rice
300g.(10½oz.) ------- baby pork ribs
6T. --minced green onion
2T. ---------- minced ginger

1T.each ---- minced garlic, fermented black soy beans (wet)
1 ---------- red chili pepper

1
• 2T.corn starch
• 1t.cooking wine
• ¼t.each salt, soy sauce

2
• 1C.water
• 3T.soy sauce
• 2t.sugar
• 1t.cooking wine
• ⅛t.pepper

1 Wash the pork ribs and chop into small serving pieces. Marinate ribs in **1**. Discard seeds from red chili pepper and mince.
2 Heat the wok, add 2C. oil, fry ribs until golden, remove.
3 Keep 1T. oil in the wok and heat, stir fry garlic, red chili pepper, black soy beans, and 3T. green onion until fragrant. Add **2** and bring to a boil. Pour over ribs, and steam over high heat for 50 minutes. Pour over rice, sprinkle on the rest of green onion and serve.
■ Vegetables may be served with the rice for added nutrition.

苦瓜排骨飯 • *Pork Ribs and Bitter Melon Rice*

白飯 -------------- １０００公克	小排骨 -------------- ５００公克
苦瓜（１條）------ ６００公克	

❶
- 地瓜粉 -------------- ２大匙
- 酒、醬油、蒜末各１大匙
- 糖 -------------------- １小匙
- 味精 ----------------- ½小匙
- 鹽 ------------------- ¼小匙
- 五香粉、麻油 ---- 各少許

❷
- 水 ---------------------- ３杯
- 鹽、糖 ----------- 各１小匙
- 味精 ----------------- ½小匙

1 苦瓜去籽，切成１×３公分之條狀，小排骨加❶料醃１５分鐘，備用。

2 鍋熱入油４杯燒至七分熱（１６０℃），入苦瓜炸至熟透取出，再入排骨炸至金黃色，撈出瀝油，將排骨加❷料煮開備用。

3 取四個扣碗，先排入苦瓜，再入排骨及湯汁，入鍋大火蒸４０分鐘，取出扣於白飯上即可。

1000g.(2⅕lb.) cooked rice
600g.(1⅓lb.) --------- bitter melon (one whole)

500g.(1⅒lb.)---baby pork ribs

❶
- •2T.sweet potato flour
- •1T.each cooking wine, soy sauce, minced garlic
- •1t.sugar
- •¼t.salt
- •dash of each: five spices powder, sesame oil

❷
- •3C.water
- •1t.each salt, sugar

1 Discard seeds from the bitter melon, cut it into 1 cm x 3 cm (⅖" x 1⅕") strips. Marinate ribs in ❶ for 15 minutes.

2 Heat the wok, add 4C. oil and heat to 160℃ (320°F); deep fry melon until cooked, remove. Then deep fry ribs until golden, remove and drain. Bring ribs and ❷ to boil.

3 In four serving bowls, arrange bitter melon strips, place a layer of ribs and some sauce. Steam over high heat for 40 minutes. Invert the bowls onto four rice platters and serve.

紅燒牛腩飯 • *Soy Braised Beef Rice*

白飯 -------------- 1000公克	紅辣椒 ---------------------- 2條
牛腩、白蘿蔔---各300公克	蔥綠末 -------------------- 3大匙
蔥白 ------------------------ 6段	黑豆瓣醬、蒜末 ------ 各1大匙
薑片 ------------------------ 6片	

1
- 水 ---------------------- 6杯
- 醬油 ------------------ 3大匙
- 酒 --------------------- 1大匙
- 糖 -------------------- ½大匙
- 花椒 ------------------ ¼小匙
- 八角 ------------------ 1顆

2
- 水 --------------------- 1大匙
- 太白粉 --------------- ½大匙

1 紅辣椒去籽切片，牛腩切2公分之塊狀，白蘿蔔去皮切大塊備用。

2 鍋熱入油2大匙燒熱，炒香蔥白、薑、蒜、紅辣椒後，再入豆瓣醬炒勻，續入牛腩拌炒，隨即入 **1** 料煮開，改小火煮1小時，再入白蘿蔔續煮1小時，以 **2** 料芶芡，灑上蔥綠末，再淋於白飯上即可。

1000g.(2⅕lb.) cooked rice
300g.(10½oz.) each - beef brisket, turnip
6 sections ---- green onion (white part)
6 slices -------------- ginger

2 --------- red chili peppers
3T. -- minced green onion (green part)
1T.each -- dark brown soy bean paste, minced garlic

1
- 6C.water
- 3T.soy sauce
- 1T.cooking wine
- ½T.sugar
- ¼t.Szechwan pepper corn
- 1 star anise

2
- 1T.water
- ½T.corn starch

1 Discard seeds from red chili peppers and slice. Cut beef into 2 cm (⅘") serving squares. Peel turnip and cut into large serving pieces.

2 Heat the wok, add 2T. oil and heat; stir fry green onion sections, ginger, garlic, and red chili peppers until fragrant. Evenly mix in soy bean paste, add beef, fry. Pour in **1** and bring to a boil, turn heat to low and simmer for 1 hour. Add turnip and simmer for another 1 hour. Thicken with **2**, sprinkle on minced green onion. Pour over rice and serve.

番茄牛肉燴飯 • *Tomato and Beef Rice*

白飯 -------------- 1000公克
番茄 ----------------- 440公克

牛肉 ----------------- 300公克
洋蔥、豌豆莢 ------各80公克

1┌ 水 ------------------- 2大匙
　　│ 油、太白粉、醬油 --------
　　│ ----------------- 各1大匙
　　│ 酒 ------------------- ½大匙
　　└ 小蘇打 --------------- ½小匙

2┌ 水 ----------------- 2杯
　　│ 糖 ----------------- 3大匙
　　│ 醬油、番茄醬 --各2大匙
　　│ 酒、鹽、麻油 -- 各1小匙
　　└ 味精 ----------------- ½小匙

3┌ 水 ------------------- 2大匙
　　└ 太白粉 ------------- 1大匙

1 洋蔥、番茄各切塊，豌豆莢去老纖維，牛肉逆紋切薄片入 **1** 料
　醃30分鐘。
2 鍋熱入油3杯燒熱，入牛肉過油至變色，隨即撈起，留油2大匙
　燒熱，入洋蔥炒香，續入番茄及**2**料煮開，改小火續煮5分鐘，
　入豌豆莢，並以**3**料芶芡，再入牛肉拌勻，淋於白飯上即可。

1000g.(2⅕lb.) cooked rice
440g.(15½oz.)--tomatoes
300g.(10½oz.) --------beef

80g.(2⅘oz.) each -onion, snow pea pods

1┌ •2T.water
　　│ •1T.each oil, corn
　　│ starch, soy sauce
　　│ •½T.cooking wine
　　└ •½t.baking soda

2┌ •2C.water
　　│ •3T.sugar
　　│ •2T.each soy sauce,
　　│ ketchup
　　│ •1t.each cooking
　　└ wine, salt, sesame oil

3┌ •2T.water
　　└ •1T.corn starch

1 Cut onion and tomatoes into serving pieces. Discard tough fibers on pea pods. Thinly slice beef against the grain, marinate in **1** for 30 minutes.
2 Heat the wok, add 3C. oil and heat; soak beef in hot oil until color pales, remove immediately and drain. Keep 2T. oil in the wok and heat, stir fry onion until fragrant. Add tomatoes and **2**, bring to a boil; turn heat to low and simmer for 5 minutes. Add pea pods, thicken with **3**. Mix in beef evenly. Pour over rice and serve.

香菇雞煲飯 • *Mushrooms and Chicken Rice in Pot*

雞腿 ---------------- 600公克	蔥段 --------------------- 12段	600g.(1⅓lb.) chicken legs	8g.(¼oz.) ------ dried black
蓬萊米 ------------- 300公克	薑片 ----------------------- 6片	300g.(10½oz.) ------- short	mushrooms
香菇 -------------------- 8公克		grain rice	12 sections -- green onion
			6 slices --------------- ginger

1
- 醬油 --------------- 4 大匙
- 水 ------------------ 3 大匙
- 太白粉 ------------- 2 小匙
- 鹽、糖、酒、麻油 --------
  ------------------- 各 1 小匙
- 黑胡椒粉、味精 各¼小匙

2
- 油 -------------------- 1 小匙
- 鹽 -------------------- ⅛小匙

1
- 4T.soy sauce
- 3T.water
- 2t.corn starch
- 1t.each salt, sugar, cooking wine, sesame oil
- ¼t.black pepper

2
- 1t.oil
- ⅛t.salt

1 雞腿洗淨去骨，切成 4×4 公分塊狀，加蔥段、薑片及 **1** 料醃 1 小時，香菇泡軟洗淨去蒂對切，與醃好的雞肉拌勻備用。

2 米洗淨瀝乾，入砂鍋中，加水 1¾杯及 **2** 料以大火煮開，改小火蓋鍋煮15分鐘後，入香菇、雞肉舖勻再蓋鍋，續以小火煮40分鐘熄火，再燜10分鐘即可。

■ 小火煨飯時須不時轉動砂鍋，使受熱均勻。

1 Wash chicken legs and remove the bones, cut into 4 cm x 4 cm (1½" x 1½") serving pieces; marinate with green onion, ginger, and **1** for one hour. Soften mushrooms in warm water, discard stems, and cut into halves, mix into the chicken marinade.

2 Wash rice, place in a ceramic pot, add 1¾C. water and **2**; bring to a boil over high heat, cover with lid, simmer over low heat for 15 minutes. Spread mushrooms and chicken over rice, cover with lid, continue to simmer over low heat for 40 minutes. Turn off heat, keeping the lid on for 10 more minutes. Serve.

■ The pot must be moved and turned constantly during simmering, in order to obtain heat evenly on all sides.

酸菜牛肉煲飯 • *Sour Mustard and Beef Rice in Pot*

蓬萊米 ---------------- 3 0 0 公克　　酸菜 ------------------ 1 0 0 公克
牛肉 ------------------ 2 0 0 公克　　糖 ------------------------- 1 小匙

1
┌ 水 ---------------------- 2 大匙
│ 醬油 ------------------- 1 大匙
│ 太白粉 ---------------- ½大匙
│ 酒 ---------------------- 1 小匙
│ 糖 ---------------------- ½小匙
└ 小蘇打 --------------- ¼小匙

2
┌ 水 ---------------------- 2 大匙
│ 醬油 ------------------- 1 大匙
└ 太白粉 --------------- 2 小匙

1 牛肉洗淨切薄片，以 **1** 料醃 1 0 分鐘後分成 3 等份，酸菜洗淨
　 切薄片備用。
2 鍋熱入油 1 大匙燒熱，入酸菜炒香，續入糖拌炒均勻，分成 2 等
　 份備用。
3 米洗淨瀝乾水分，入砂鍋中加水 1 ½ 杯煮開，改小火蓋鍋煮 1 5
　 分鐘後，第一層先舖上 1 份牛肉，第二層舖 1 份酸菜，第三層再
　 舖上牛肉，第四層舖上剩下的酸菜，第五層舖上牛肉後，淋上 **2**
　 料蓋鍋以小火續煮 3 0 分鐘，熄火再燜 1 0 分鐘即可。
■ 小火燜飯時須不時轉動砂鍋，使受熱均勻。

300g.(10½oz.) ------- short grain rice
200g.(7oz.)------------ beef

100g.(3½lb.) ---------- sour mustard
1t. --------------------- sugar

1
• 2T.water
• 1T.soy sauce
• ½T.corn starch
• 1t.cooking wine
• ½t.sugar
• ¼t.baking soda

2
• 2T.water
• 1T.soy sauce
• 2t.corn starch

1 Wash beef and slice thin, marinate with **1** for 10 minutes; divide into 3 portions. Wash sour mustard and slice thin.
2 Heat the wok, add 1T. oil and heat; stir fry sour mustard until fragrant. Mix in sugar. Divide into 2 portions.
3 Wash rice and drain. Place rice in a ceramic pot, add 1½C. water and bring to a boil; turn heat to low, cover with lid, and simmer for 15 minutes. Spread one layer of beef on the rice, then a layer of sour mustard alternatively, ending with beef layer on top. Pour **2** over beef, cover with lid, and simmer over low heat for 30 minutes. Turn off heat and keep the lid on for 10 more minutes. Serve.
■ The pot must be moved and turned constantly during simmering in order to obtain heat evenly on all sides.

臘味煲飯 • *Chinese Sausage and Bacon Rice in Pot*

蓮萊米 -------------- ３００公克　　廣式香腸、臘肉、青江菜 ------
　　　　　　　　　　　　　　　-------------------- 各１００公克

1⌈ 水 ---------------------- １¾杯　　　**2**⌈ 麻油 ------------------ ½小匙
　├ 醬油 ---------------- １大匙　　　　　└ 鹽 --------------------- ⅛小匙
　└ 油 -------------------- １小匙

1 廣式香腸以熱水浸泡５分鐘後，洗淨，與臘肉均切薄片備用。

2 米洗淨瀝乾水分，加 **1** 料入砂鍋中煮開，改小火蓋鍋煮１５分
鐘後，入廣式香腸、臘肉蓋鍋以小火煮４０分鐘熄火，再燜１０
分鐘。

3 青江菜洗淨，入滾水中燙熟，撈出瀝乾，與 **2** 料拌勻，放在煲
飯上即可。

■ 小火煨飯時須不時轉動砂鍋，使受熱均勻。

300g.(10½oz.) ------- short
grain rice

100g.(3½lb.) each ---------
Cantonese sausage,
Chinese bacon, bok choy

1⌈ • 1¾C.water　　　　**2**⌈ • ½t.sesame oil
　├ • 1T.soy sauce　　　　　└ • ⅛t.salt
　└ • 1t.oil

1 Soak Cantonese sausage in hot water for 5 minutes,
rinse clean. Cut both sausage and bacon into thin
slices.

2 Rinse rice and drain. Place rice and **1** in a ceramic pot,
bring to a boil. Turn heat to low, cover with lid, and
simmer for 15 minutes. Add sausage and bacon, cover
and simmer for another 40 minutes. Turn off heat,
keep the lid on for 10 more minutes before serving.

3 Wash bok choy, cook in boiling water; lift out and
drain. Mix well with **2**. Use as the garnish around rice.
Serve.

■ The pot must be moved and turned constantly during
simmering in order to heat evenly.

肉燥飯 • *Ground Pork Sauce Rice*

白飯 ------------- 1000公克	紅蔥頭 ------------- 150公克
絞肉 ----------------- 300公克	香菇 -------------------- 10公克

❶
- 水 ----------------------- 3 杯
- 醬油 ----------------- 5 大匙
- 冰糖 ----------------- 1 小匙
- 鹽 ---------------------- ¼小匙
- 五香粉、肉桂粉 各⅛小匙
- 八角 -------------------- 1 顆

1　香菇泡軟去蒂，洗淨瀝乾水分切小丁，紅蔥頭去皮、頭、尾並洗淨後切薄片備用。

2　鍋熱入油 5 大匙燒熱，入紅蔥頭片炒至呈金黃色，續入香菇丁炒香後，再入絞肉炒勻，隨即入 **❶** 料煮開，改小火燉煮 3 0 分鐘後，起鍋淋於白飯上即可。

1000g.(2⅕lb.) cooked rice
300g.(10½oz.) ---- ground pork

150g.(5⅓oz.) - red shallots
10g.(⅓oz.) ----- dried black mushrooms

❶
- • 3C. water
- • 5T. soy sauce
- • 1t. crystal sugar
- • ¼t. salt
- • ⅛t. each five spices powder, cinnamon powder
- • 1 star anise

1　Soften black mushrooms in warm water, discard stems; rinse clean, drain and dice. Peel shallots, trim off ends; rinse and slice thin.

2　Heat the wok, add 5T. oil and heat; stir fry shallots until golden. Stir in mushrooms and fry until fragrant. Add pork, fry evenly. Pour in **❶** and bring to a boil, turn heat to low and simmer for 30 minutes. Pour over rice and serve.

米花糖

• Popped Rice Candy

米花糖 • *Popped Rice Candy*

乾的熟糯米 --------- 3 0 0 公克
長方形模型 ------------------ 1 個

1 ⎡ 去皮花生 -------- 3 0 公克
　　 ⎢ 油蔥酥 ------------- 6 大匙
　　 ⎣ 蒜茸酥 ------------- 1 大匙

2 ⎡ 麥芽糖 ---------- 9 0 公克
　　 ⎢ 細糖 -------------------- 1 杯
　　 ⎢ 水 ----------------------- ⅓杯
　　 ⎣ 鹽 -------------------- ½小匙

1 油 1 2 杯加熱至 2 0 0 ℃，入乾的熟糯米炸至膨發，撈起瀝乾油分，與 **1** 料混合均勻備用。
2 模型先均勻地擦上一層油備用。
3 **2** 料小火煮成糖漿（圖 1）（煮至糖漿滴在冷水中成柔軟之圓球狀即可），趁熱倒入 **1** 項材料攪拌（圖 2）均勻，再倒入抹油之模型中並壓平（圖 3），待涼再切塊即可。
■ 若買不到現成乾的熟糯米，可自己製作，做法如下：
　圓糯米 6 0 0 公克煮熟成糯米飯，再將糯米飯刨鬆並均勻地鋪在烤盤上，入 7 0 ℃烤箱烤至米粒全乾，烤時須不時翻攪，讓米粒不要結團使散成粒狀。

300g.(10½oz.) ----------------- dried cooked glutinous rice
1 --- rectangular mold

1 ⎡ •30g.(1oz.) peeled peanuts
　　 ⎢ •6T. fried shallot flakes
　　 ⎣ •1T. crispy garlic crumb

2 ⎡ •90g.(3⅕oz.) maltose
　　 ⎢ •1C. sugar
　　 ⎢ •⅓C. water
　　 ⎣ •½t. salt

1 Heat 12C. oil to 200℃ (392°F), deep fry rice until popped. Lift out and drain. Mix well with **1** .
2 Grease mold with a thin film of oil.
3 Melt **2** over low heat into syrup (illus.1) (syrup should form into a soft ball when droped into cold water), mix well with step **1** ingredients while syrup is still warm (illus. 2). Pour into greased mold and press evenly (illus. 3). Cut into squares when cooled.
■ If you cannot find dried cooked glutinous rice, it can be made at home as follows:
Cook 600g.(1⅓lb.) short grain glutinous rice until done. Loosen rice and spread evenly onto a baking sheet. Bake in 70℃ (158°F) oven until rice is dry. Stir rice often during baking to avoid sticking.

1

2

3

八寶飯 • *Sweet Rice Pudding with Eight Treasures*

圓糯米 ------------- ２００公克	豬油 ----------------- １小匙	200g.(7oz.) ---short grain glutinous rice	50g.(1¾oz.) ----sweet red bean paste
豆沙 ------------------ ５０公克			1t. -----------------------lard

1 [
蜜花豆 ---------- ３０公克
紅棗 ------------- １５公克
龍眼乾、木瓜蜜餞（紅、綠） ---------- 各１０公克
葡萄乾 ------------- ５公克
鳳梨片 ----------------- ２片
桔餅 ------------------- １個
]

2 [
糖 ------------------- ３大匙
豬油 ---------------- １大匙
]

1 •30g.(1oz.) sweet red beans
•15g.(½oz.) dried Chinese dates
•10g.(⅓oz.) each dried longans, candied papayas (red, green)
•5g.(⅕oz.) raisins
•2 candied pineapples
•1 candied kumquat

2 •3T.sugar
•1T.lard

1 取一中碗，先塗抹上豬油後，再把 **1** 料整齊地排在碗底備用。

2 糯米煮成糯米飯，趁熱入 **2** 料拌勻，取一半糯米飯先放入排好圖案（圖１）之碗內，中間略成凹狀，填入豆沙（圖２），再將另一半糯米飯，舖在豆沙上攤平壓緊，再入鍋蒸３０分鐘取出，倒扣於盤上即可。

■ 八寶之種類可依個人喜好而變換。

1 Grease a medium sized bowl with lard, arrange all materials in **1** neatly onto the bottom of the bowl.

2 Cook rice. Mix in **2** while rice still warm. Place half of rice into the bowl (illus. 1), make a shallow dent in the middle; fill the dent with red bean paste (illus. 2) and spread the rest of the rice over evenly. Steam for 30 minutes, invert onto a plate and serve hot.

■ Eight treasure sweets may be changed according to personal taste.

1

2

冰糖蓮藕 • *Stuffed Lotus Root Dessert*

蓮藕（2節）------ 4 3 0公克　　冰糖 -------------------------- 2 杯
圓糯米 -------------- 1 0 0公克

1⎡ 水 ---------------------- 1 杯　　**2**⎡ 水 --------------------- 2 小匙
　⎢ 冰糖 --------------- 3⅓大匙　　　⎣ 太白粉 -------------- 1 小匙
　⎣ 蜂蜜 ----------------- 1 大匙

1 糯米洗淨，蓮藕外皮刷乾淨後，從藕節的一端切開，再由藕面之孔隙塞入糯米（圖1），塞糯米的時候須不停上下輕微震動，以利米粒之充填，約 7 分滿後，將切開的蓋子蓋回，並用牙籤固定（圖2）。
2 蓮藕入電鍋內鍋中，加水淹過蓮藕，入電鍋煮 3 小時，再加冰糖續煮 3 0分鐘，取出切片排盤。
3 **1** 料煮開，以 **2** 料芶芡，再淋於藕片上即可。

430g.(15⅕oz.) - lotus root (2 links)

100g.(3½oz.) - short grain glutinous rice

2C. ------------ crystal sugar

1⎡ •1C.water
　⎢ •3⅓T.crystal sugar
　⎣ •1T.honey

2⎡ •2t.water
　⎣ •1t.corn starch

1 Wash rice. Brush clean the outer skin of lotus root, cut open from the thicker end. Stuff rice into the holes (illus. 1), shake the root up and down during the stuffing to slide in the rice. Fill up to 70%, and cover with the lid piece, staple with toothpicks. (illus. 2)
2 Place stuffed lotus roots into the inner pot of a rice cooker, cover with water; steam for 3 hours. Add crystal sugar and continue steaming for 30 more minutes. Slice and arrange on a plate.
3 Bring **1** to a boil, thicken with **2**. Pour over stuffed lotus roots and serve.

1

2

糯米捲尖 • *Stuffed Sweet Rice Pastry*

圓糯米 ------------ 300公克	細糖 --------------------- 3大匙	300g.(10½oz.) short grain glutinous rice	1C. ------------ corn starch
豆沙 -------------- 200公克	豬油 --------------------- 2大匙	200g.(7oz.) ----- sweet red bean paste	3T. --------------------- sugar
太白粉 ---------------- 1杯	豆腐皮 --------------------- 2張		2T. ----------------------- lard
			2 ------------ bean curd skin

1 糯米煮成糯米飯，趁熱拌入細糖及豬油，與豆沙均分成2等份。

2 豆腐皮鋪平，取1份糯米飯鋪在豆腐皮上，壓成10×20公分之長方形，1份豆沙揉成長條，放在糯米飯中間，然後捲起成長條筒狀，另1份依此方式作好。

3 鍋熱入油6杯燒至六分熱（140℃），將糯米捲入油鍋中，炸至金黃色撈起，切成3公分長段即可。

1 Cook rice. Mix in sugar and lard while still warm. Divide rice and sweet red bean paste into 2 equal portions.

2 Spread one portion of rice over one sheet of bean curd skin, press into 10 cm x 20 cm (4" x 7⅘") long rectangle. Roll one portion of red bean paste into one long strip. Place one strip in the middle of rice, roll it into cylinder shape. Make the other portion the same way.

3 Heat the wok, add 6C. oil and heat to 140℃ (284℉); fry rice pastries until golden, remove. Cut into 3 cm (1⅕") long sections and serve.

廣東粥 • *Cantonese Congee*

蓬萊米 -------------- ３００公克	魷魚（乾）----------- １５公克	300g.(10½oz.) ------short grain rice	30g.(1oz.) -----deep fried Chinese cruller (illus. 1)
雞肝 ----------------- ２１０公克	高湯 ----------------- １２杯	210g.(7⅖oz.)chicken liver	15g.(½oz.) dried cuttlefish
雞胸肉 -------------- １５０公克	玉米醬 ----------------- １杯	150g.(5⅓oz.) ------chicken breast	12C. -------------------stock
油條（圖１）-------- ３０公克	蔥末 ----------------- ５大匙		1C. -----corn, cream style
			5T. --minced green onion

1
┌ 太白粉 ------------- １大匙
│ 鹽、味精 --------- 各½小匙
└ 蛋 ----------------- ½個

2
┌ 鹽 ----------------- １½小匙
│ 味精 ----------------- １小匙
└ 胡椒粉 ------------- ½小匙

1
┌ •1T.corn starch
│ •½t.salt
└ •½ egg

2
┌ •1½t.salt
└ •½t.pepper

1 雞肝洗淨入開水川燙後切小丁，魷魚洗淨切５×０．５公分長條狀，入熱水中泡１５分鐘，雞胸肉洗淨剁成泥狀，入 **1** 料醃約１０分鐘，油條切小塊（圖２）備用。

2 米洗淨入高湯及玉米醬大火煮開，改中火煮１０分鐘，續入魷魚煮１０分鐘，最後加入雞肝、雞泥及 **2** 料煮熟，起鍋前灑上蔥末及油條即可。

1 Wash chicken liver, parboil in boiling water, and dice. Wash cuttlefish, cut into 5cm x 0.5 cm (2 " x ⅕") long strips, soak in hot water for 15 minutes. Finely chop chicken breast to mashed paste, marinate with **1** for 10 minutes. Cut cruller into small serving cubes (illus. 2).

2 Rinse rice, add stock and corn, bring to a boil over high heat. Simmer over medium heat for 10 minutes. Add cuttlefish and cook for 10 minutes. Stir in liver, mashed chicken, and **2**, cook until done. Sprinkle on green onion and cruller. Serve.

1

2

甘薯粥 • *Yam Congee*

紅心甘薯 ----------- ４００公克　　蓬萊米 -------------- ２５０公克

1 甘薯去皮洗淨，切成滾刀塊，米洗淨備用。
2 甘薯、米和水１３杯入鍋以大火煮開後，改小火續煮２５分鐘即可。

400g.(14oz.) -----red yam　250g.(8⁴/₅oz.) --------short
(net weight)　　　　　　grain rice

1 Wash and skin yam, cut into slanted pieces. Rinse rice.
2 Add yam and rice in 13C. water. Bring to a boil over high heat, then simmer over low heat for 25 minutes. Serve.

四人份　**serve 4**

臘八粥 • *La-Ba Sweet Winter Congee*

糯米 ----------------- １３５公克　　**①**⎡ 薏仁、紅豆、綠豆、蓮子
熟花生 ----------------- ７５公克　　　　--------------各７５公克
紅棗 ----------------- １６顆　　　　　⎣ 栗子 --------------- １６顆
糖 ----------------------- １杯

1 **①**料洗淨入水１５杯，大火煮開，改小火煮１０分鐘後，續入洗淨的糯米煮３５分鐘，再入紅棗煮１０分鐘，最後入糖及花生再煮１０分鐘即可。
■ 八寶的材料可依個人之喜好更改或增減。

135g.(4³/₄oz.) --- glutinous
rice
75g.(2²/₃oz.) --------boiled
peanuts
16 ------dried Chinese red
dates
1C. --------------------sugar

①⎡•75g.(2²/₃oz.) each pearl-barley, red beans, mung beans, lotus seeds
⎣•16 chestnuts

1 Wash **①**, add 15C. water, bring to a boil over high heat. Simmer over low heat for 10 minutes. Add rinsed rice and simmer for 35 minutes. Add red dates and simmer for 10 minutes. Stir in sugar and peanuts, simmer for 10 minutes. Serve.
■ Materials may be changed according to personal taste.

　四人份　**serve 4**

雞絨南瓜粥 •*Pumpkin Congee*

南瓜 ------------------- 250公克
蓬萊米 -------------- 200公克
雞胸肉 -------------- 150公克
薑絲 --------------------- 10公克

1 ┌ 鹽 ----------------- 1½小匙
│ 酒 ----------------- 1小匙
└ 味精、胡椒粉 --- 各¼小匙

1 南瓜去皮、籽洗淨磨成泥狀; 雞胸肉洗淨剁成泥狀備用。
2 米洗淨入水9杯，大火煮開，改小火煮20分鐘後，續入南瓜、雞泥、薑絲再煮8分鐘，最後入**1**料拌勻即可。

250g.(8⁴/₅oz.) ---pumpkin
200g.(7oz.) ---short grain rice
150g.(5⅓oz.) ------chicken breast
10g.(⅓oz.) -------shredded ginger

1 ┌ •1½t.salt
│ •1t.cooking wine
└ •¼t.pepper

1 Skin pumpkin, discard seeds, and mash to paste. Rinse chicken breast and finely chop into mashed paste.
2 Rinse rice, add 9C. water and bring to a boil over high heat. Simmer over low heat for 20 minutes. Add mashed pumpkin, mashed chicken, and ginger, simmer for 8 more minutes. Season with **1**, mix well and serve.

四人份　**serve 4**

虱目魚粥 •*Milk Fish Congee*

虱目魚（中段）--- 600公克
蓬萊米 -------------- 300公克
薑絲 -------------------- 40公克
芹菜末 ----------------------- ¾杯

1 ┌ 酒 -------------------- 2大匙
│ 鹽 ------------------- 1大匙
└ 味精 ----------------- 1小匙

1 虱目魚洗淨，切圓圈段，入開水中川燙隨即撈出備用。
2 米洗淨加水16杯，大火煮開，改中火煮15分鐘，續入薑絲及虱目魚再煮5分鐘，入**1**料拌勻，起鍋後灑上芹菜末即可。

600g.(1⅓lb.) -----milk fish (middle section)
300g.(10½oz.) -------short grain rice

¾C. ---------minced celery
40g.(1²/₅oz.) -----shredded ginger

1 ┌ •2T.cooking wine
└ •1T.salt

1 Wash milk fish, cut into round serving pieces; parboil in boiling water and lift out to drain.
2 Rinse rice, add 16C. water and bring to a boil over high heat; simmer over medium heat for 15 minutes. Add ginger and fish, cook for 5 minutes. Mix in **1** evenly. Sprinkle with celery and serve.

四人份　**serve 4**

三元及第粥

·*Luxurious Pork Congee*

四人份　**serve 4**

52

三元及第粥 • *Luxurious Pork Congee*

蓬萊米 -------------- 300公克	300g.(10½oz.) -------------------------------- short grain rice
豬肝 ------------------ 200公克	200g.(7oz.) -- pork liver
豬腰 ------------------ 120公克	120g.(4¼oz.) -------------------------------------- pork kidney
里肌肉 --------------- 70公克	70g.(2½oz.)-- pork fillet
油條 ------------------ 30公克	30g.(1oz.) ----------------------- deep fried Chinese cruller
蔥絲 ------------------ 20公克	20g.(²/₃oz.) ------------------------- shredded green onion
香菜末 --------------- 15公克	15g.(½oz.) --------------------------------- minced coriander
高湯 ----------------------- 10杯	10C. --- stock

1 醬油、水、太白粉 --------
　　　 -------------------- 各1大匙

2 鹽、味精、麻油 各¼小匙
胡椒粉 -------------- ⅛小匙

3 酒 ------------------- 1大匙
鹽 ------------------- 1小匙
味精、胡椒粉 --- 各½小匙

1 豬腰橫切開，除去內面白筋（圖1），洗淨切片泡冷水約10分鐘瀝乾（圖2），豬肝切片，與豬腰均入 **1** 料醃10分鐘，里肌肉切薄片入 **2** 料醃10分鐘，油條切小塊備用。
2 米洗淨入高湯10杯，大火煮開，改中火續煮15分鐘後，入豬腰、豬肝及肉片煮熟，最後入 **3** 料調味，起鍋前再灑上蔥絲、香菜及油條即可。

1 •1T.each soy sauce, water, corn starch

2 •¼t.each salt, sesame oil •⅛t.pepper

3 •1T.cooking wine •1t.salt •½t.pepper

1 Slice the kidney horizontally in half; trim off white sinews from the center (illus. 1), wash and soak in cold water for 10 minutes, drain (illus. 2). Slice pork liver, marinate with kidney in **1** for 10 minutes. Thinly slice pork and marinate in **2** for 10 minutes. Cut cruller into small serving cubes.
2 Rinse rice, add 10C. stock and bring to a boil over high heat, simmer over medium heat for 15 minutes. Stir in kidney, liver, and pork, cook until done. Season with **3**. Sprinkle on green onion, coriander, and cruller. Serve.

1

2

滑蛋牛肉粥 • *Soft Egg and Beef Congee*

蓬萊米 -------------- 3 0 0公克		油條 -------------------- 1 0公克	
牛里肌 -------------- 1 1 0公克		蛋 ----------------------------- 1個	
薑絲、蔥絲 --------- 各2 0公克		香菜 ----------------------------- 少許	

1
- 水 -------------------- 2大匙
- 油 -------------------- 1大匙
- 醬油 ------------------ ½大匙
- 太白粉 -------------- 1小匙

2
- 鹽 ------------------ 1⅓大匙
- 味精、胡椒粉 --- 各½小匙

1 牛里肌洗淨，逆紋切片入 **1** 料醃1 0分鐘，油條切小塊備用。

2 米洗淨加水1 0杯，大火煮開，改中火煮1 5分鐘，續入牛肉、薑絲、蔥絲煮開，最後入打散之蛋液及 **2** 料拌勻，起鍋後灑上油條及香菜即可。

■ 若無油條可以炸過之餛飩皮取代。

300g.(10½oz.) ------- short grain rice
110g.(4oz.) ----- beef fillet
20g.(⅔oz.)each ------------ shredded green onion, shredded ginger

10g.(⅓oz.) ------ deep fried Chinese cruller
1 ------------------------- egg
dash of --------- coriander

1
- •2T.water
- •1T.oil
- •½T.soy sauce
- •1t.corn starch

2
- •1⅓T.salt
- •½t.pepper

1 Rinse beef, slice thin, marinate in **1** for 10 minutes. Cut cruller to small serving cubes.

2 Rinse rice, add 10C. water; bring to a boil over high heat, simmer over medium heat for 15 minutes. Add beef, ginger, and green onion; bring to a boil again. Then stir in beaten egg and **2** , mix well. Sprinkle on cruller and coriander. Serve.

■ Cruller may be replaced by deep fried wonton wrapper.

生菜牛肉粥 • *Lettuce and Beef Congee*

生菜 ------------------ 2 5 0公克　　蓬萊米 -------------- 2 0 0公克
牛里肌 -------------- 2 2 5公克

1[醬油 ----------------- 1 大匙
　 太白粉、酒 ------ 各½大匙

2[鹽 ------------------- 1 小匙
　 味精 ----------------- ⅙小匙

1 牛肉切薄片入 **1** 料醃１０分鐘；生菜洗淨瀝乾切３×４公分備用。
2 米洗淨加水８杯，大火煮開，改小火煮２０分鐘後，續入牛肉煮開，熄火再加生菜及 **2** 料拌勻即可。
■ 食用時可依個人喜好添加胡椒粉。

250g.(8⅘oz.) ------ lettuce　200g.(7oz.) --- short grain
225g.(8oz.) ----- beef fillet　rice

1[•1T.soy sauce
　 •½T.each corn starch,
　 cooking wine

2 •1t.salt

1 Thinly slice beef and marinate in **1** for 10 minutes. Wash lettuce and cut into 3 cm x 4 cm (1⅕" x 1½") long strips.
2 Rinse rice, add 8C. water and bring to a boil, simmer over low heat for 20 minutes. Add beef and bring to a boil again. Turn off heat, mix in lettuce and season with **2**. Serve.
■ Pepper may be added during serving, depending on personal taste.

皮蛋瘦肉粥 • *Pork Congee with Thousand-year-old Eggs*

蓬萊米 ------------- ２５０公克	芹菜末 -------------------- ３大匙
絞肉 ----------------- １５０公克	玉米醬 ----------------------- １杯
油條 -------------------- １０公克	皮蛋 ------------------------- ３個

1┌ 鹽 --------------------- ２小匙
　　│ 味精 ----------------- １小匙
　　└ 胡椒粉 --------------- ¹/₂小匙

1 皮蛋去殼切小丁，油條切小塊備用。
2 米洗淨加水１４杯，大火煮開，改中火煮２５分鐘，續入玉米醬、絞肉、皮蛋及 **1** 料煮熟，起鍋後灑上油條及芹菜末即可。

250g.(8⁴/₅oz.) -------- short grain rice
150g.(5¹/₃oz.) ------ ground pork
3T. ---- ------ minced celery

10g.(¹/₃oz.) ------ deep fried Chinese cruller
1C. ------ cream style corn
3 ------- thousand-year-old eggs

1┌ •2t.salt
　　└ •¹/₂t.pepper

1 Peel off shell and dice the eggs. Cut cruller to small serving cubes.
2 Rinse rice, add 14C. water; bring to a boil over high heat, simmer over medium heat for 25 minutes. Then add corn, pork, eggs, and **1**, simmer until cooked. Sprinkle on cruller and minced celery, serve hot.

豬腸糙米粥 • *Brown Rice Congee*

豬小腸 -------------- 6 0 0 公克	糙米 ----------------- 2 7 0 公克
小排骨 -------------- 3 0 0 公克	

1
- 水 -------------------- 5 杯
- 酒 -------------------- 2 大匙
- 蔥 段 ----------------- 5 段
- 薑 片 ----------------- 2 片

2
- 酒 -------------------- 2 小匙
- 鹽 -------------------- 1 小匙
- 味精、胡椒粉 --- 各½小匙

1 豬小腸洗淨入 **1** 料川燙切段，小排骨剁小塊亦入鍋川燙再洗淨。

2 將豬小腸及洗淨之糙米加水 1 6 杯，大火煮開，續入排骨，改小火煮至米熟爛（約 7 0 分鐘），再入 **2** 料調味即可。

600g.(1⅓lb.) --- small pork intestines
300g.(10½oz.) - baby pork ribs

270g.(9½oz.) ------- brown unpolished rice

1
- •5C.water
- •2T.cooking wine
- •5 sections green onion
- •2 slices ginger

2
- •2t.cooking wine
- •1t.salt
- •½t.pepper

1 Thoroughly wash small pork intestines, parboil in **1** , remove and cut into serving sections. Chop ribs into small serving pieces, parboil in same pot, remove and rinse clean.

2 Add pork intestines and rice into 16C. water, bring to a boil. Add ribs, turn heat to low and simmer until rice is soft (about 70 minutes). Season with **2** and serve.

杏仁豆腐 • *Almond Bean Curd*

糖 -------------------- 1５０公克	什錦罐頭 -------------------- 1罐	150g.(5⅓oz.) -------- sugar	20g.(⅔oz.) ------ agar-agar
蓬萊米 ----------------- ５０公克	杏仁露 -------------------- 4 大匙	50g.(1¾oz.) --- short grain	1 can --------- fruit cocktail
洋菜 -------------------- ２０公克		rice	4T. --------- almond extract

1 ⌈ 冷開水 ----------------- 8杯
⌊ 糖 ---------------------- 1杯

1 米洗淨泡水１小時，瀝乾水分，再加水 ¾ 杯入果汁機打成米漿，
1 料調勻即為糖水備用。
2 鍋中入水６杯煮沸，再入洗淨的洋菜，煮至完全溶化，再入糖、
米漿，邊倒邊攪煮沸後熄火，淋上杏仁露，過濾再倒入模型待
涼，入冰箱冷藏２０分鐘即成杏仁豆腐。
3 將杏仁豆腐切塊，再入糖水、什錦罐頭、冰塊拌勻即可。

1 ⌈ •8C.water
⌊ •1C.sugar

1 Rinse rice and soak in water for 1 hour, drain. Add
¾C. water and puree in a blender, mix well with **1**.
2 Bring 6C. water to a boil, add washed agar-agar, boil
until agar-agar dissolved. Mix in sugar and rice puree,
stir constantly until boiled, turn off the heat. Pour in
almond extract, run through a sieve and pour in a
mold and allow to cool. Chill in refrigerator for 20
minutes.
3 Cut almond bean curd into mouthful pieces, mix in
sugar water, fruit cocktail and ice cubes. Serve.

海鮮板條 • *Seafood Rice Fettucine*

魚骨 ------------------ 150公克

150g.(5⅓oz.) --fish bones

1
[
河粉 ----------- 700公克
花枝（淨重）120公克
魚板 ------------- 70公克
劍蝦 ------------------- 8隻
]

3
[
鹽 -------------------- 1 小匙
味精 ----------------- ½小匙
糖 --------------------- ¼小匙
]

2
[
小白菜 -------- 150公克
蔥末 -------------- 3 ½大匙
]

1
[
•700g.(1½lb.) flat rice sheets
•120g.(4¼oz.) squids (net weight)
•70g.(2½oz.) kamaboko
•8 fresh shrimps
]

2
[
•150g.(5⅓oz.) baby cabbage
•3½T.minced green onion
]

3
[
•1t.salt
•¼t.sugar
]

1 河粉切2公分寬之條狀，魚板切片，花枝切花再切2 × 5公分長條狀，劍蝦剪去鬚腳，小白菜洗淨切2公分段備用。

2 魚骨入鍋川燙後，再加水9杯熬煮10分鐘撈去魚骨，再入**1**、**3**料煮開隨即加入**2**料煮熟即可。

1 Cut rice sheets into 2 cm (¾") wide noodles, slice kamaboko. Score the surface of squids and cut into 2cm x 5 cm (¾"x 2") long strips, trim off the legs of the shrimp. Wash cabbage clean and cut into 2 cm (¾") long sections.

2 Parboil fish bones, lift out. Add 9C. water with fish bones and simmer for 10 minutes, discard fish bones. Add **1** and **3** into the soup and bring to a boil. Add **2**, boil until cooked. Serve.

鼎邊銼

·Dia Bean So

鼎邊銼 • *Dia Bean So*

在來米 -------------- 150公克
紅心地瓜粉 ----------- 70公克

1
高麗菜絲 ----- 200公克
肉羹 ---------- 120公克
熟筍 ---------- 100公克
乾魷魚 ---------- 35公克
香菇、金針、芹菜 -------
------------- 各10公克
油蔥酥 ------------- 1大匙

2
高湯 -------------------- 8杯
鹽 --------------------- 2小匙
糖、麻油 -------- 各1小匙
味精 ----------------- ½小匙
胡椒粉 -------------- ¼小匙

1 在來米泡水3小時瀝乾加水至400公克打成米漿，再入紅心地瓜粉拌勻備用。

2 將鍋子燒熱，倒入六分之一的米漿（圖1）小火烘乾成圓餅狀即為鼎邊銼，全部烘完為六張圓餅（圖2）再剪成1．5×4公分之條狀（圖3）備用。

3 筍切細絲，香菇泡軟去蒂切絲，乾魷魚洗淨用剪刀剪成細絲，芹菜切末。

4 鍋熱入油2大匙燒熱，入 **1** 料炒香，續入 **2** 料煮開，再入鼎邊銼煮開即可。

150g.(5⅓oz.) ---------------------------------- long grain rice
70g.(2½oz.) ------------------------------- sweet potato flour

1
• 200g.(7oz.) shredded cabbage
• 120g.(4¼oz.) pork and fish paste dumpling
• 100g.(3½oz.) boiled or canned bamboo shoots
• 35g.(1¼oz.) dried squids
• 10g.(⅓oz.) each dried black mushrooms, golden mushrooms, celery
• 1T. fried shallot flakes

2
• 8C. stock
• 2t. salt
• 1t. each sugar, sesame oil
• ¼t. pepper

1 Soak rice in water for 3 hours, drain. Add water into the rice for a total of 400g.(14oz.) and puree in a blender, add sweet potato flour, mix well.

2 Heat a frying pan without grease, pour in ⅙ puree (illus. 1), cook dry over low heat until done. This pan cake is called Dia Bean So. Make 6 (illus. 2), then cut into 1.5 cm x 4 cm (⅗" x 1½") strips (illus. 3).

3 Shred bamboo shoots. Soften mushrooms in warm water, discard the stems, and shred. Wash squid, snip with a scissor into fine shreds. Mince celery.

4 Heat the wok, add 2T. oil and heat; stir fry **1** until fragrant. Add **2**, bring to a boil. Stir in Dia Bean So, bring to a boil again. Serve.

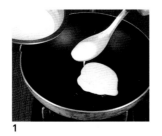
1

2

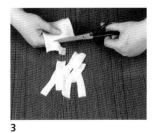
3

肉圓

• Ba Wan

肉圓 • *Ba Wan*

在來米 ----------------- 2 4 0公克	240g.(8²/₅oz.) ----------------------------------long grain rice
紅心地瓜粉 ---------- 1 6 0公克	160g.(5³/₅oz.) ----------------------------sweet potato flour
鹽 -------------------------- 1 小匙	1t. --salt
醬油碟子 ----------------- 3 0個	30 ------------------------------------small soy sauce dishes

1
- 瘦肉 ------------ 2 0 0公克
- 熟筍 ------------ 1 0 0公克
- 紅蔥頭、香菇各1 0公克

1
- •200g.(7oz.) lean pork
- •100g.(3¹/₂oz.) boiled or canned bamboo shoots
- •10g.(¹/₃oz.) each red shallots, dried black mushrooms

2
- 水 ------------------------¹/₂杯
- 醬油、麻油、太白粉 ----- ------------------- 各1 大匙
- 蠔油、糖 -------- 各1 小匙
- 鹽、黑胡椒粉 --- 各¹/₄小匙
- 味精 ------------------- 少許

2
- •¹/₂C.water
- •1T.each soy sauce,sesame oil, corn starch
- •1t.each oyster sauce, sugar
- •¹/₄t.each salt, black pepper

1 在來米洗淨泡水 3 小時後，瀝乾加水至1 2 0 0公克，打成米漿再入鹽1 小匙拌勻；香菇泡軟去蒂與其他 **1** 料切小丁備用。

2 鍋熱入油 2 大匙燒熱，入 **1** 料炒香，再入 **2** 料調味，待涼即為肉餡。

3 米漿隔水加熱（圖1）至糊狀，放涼再加入紅心地瓜粉拌勻即為肉圓外皮，分成3 0等份，醬油碟子抹油先放上半份外皮（圖2），中間再放肉餡（圖3），最後覆上半份外皮（圖4），全部做完後入蒸鍋蒸1 0分鐘即可。

1 Rinse rice and soak in water for 3 hours, drain. Add water for a total of 1200g.(2³/₅lb.), puree in a blender and add 1t. salt, mix well. Soften mushrooms in warm water, discard the stems, dice mushrooms and all other materials.

2 Heat the wok, add 2T. oil and heat; stir fry **1** until fragrant, season with **2** and allow to cool. This is the filling.

3 Put puree in a double boiler (illus. 1), heat until pasty and allow to cool. Mix in sweet potato flour evenly to create wrapper. Divide into 30 equal portions. Grease soy sauce dishes, place half portion of wrapper on the dish (illus. 2), put in the filling (illus. 3), cover with the other half of wrapper (illus. 4). Makes 30. Steam for 10 minutes.

1

2

3

4

翡翠芝麻捲 • *Jade Sesame Roll*

糯米粉、菠菜---各１５０公克　　白芝麻-----------------７０公克
太白粉-----------------７５公克　　細糖-------------------------¼杯

1 菠菜洗淨切段，加水１½杯打碎並過濾，濾汁加入糯米粉、太白粉拌勻成粉漿，再倒入已塗油的平盤內，約０‧３公分之厚度，水開入鍋大火蒸５分鐘，取出放涼即為粿粉皮備用。

2 鍋熱入白芝麻炒至金黃色，取出趁熱搗碎，再加入糖拌勻即為芝麻粉。

3 將芝麻粉均勻地灑在粿粉皮上捲成圓筒狀，再切成４公分長條即可。

150g.(5⅓oz.) each --------
glutinous rice flour,
spinach
75g.(2⅔oz.) -- corn starch

70g.(2½oz.) ----------white
sesame seeds
¼C. --------------------sugar

1 Wash spinach and cut into sections, add 1½C. water and puree in a blender. Run through a sieve and add glutinous rice flour, corn starch, mix well. Pour into a greased flat pan, about 0.3 cm (1/10 ") thick. Bring water to a boil and steam over high heat for 5 minutes. Remove and allow to cool. This is the jade wrapper.

2 Heat the wok, stir fry sesame seeds until golden. Crush while still warm. Mix in sugar. This is the filling.

3 Sprinkle the filling evenly on the wrapper, roll into a cylinder. Cut into 4 cm (1½") long sections and serve.

臘味蘿蔔糕 • *Cantonese Turnip Cake*

白蘿蔔絲 -------- 1 2 0 0公克		玻璃紙 ---------------------- 1 張

1
| 在來米 -------- 4 8 0公克 |
| 蓬萊米 -------- 1 2 0公克 |

3
| 鹽 ------------------- 1 大匙 |
| 胡椒粉、味精 -- 各1 小匙 |

2
| 廣式香腸、紅蔥頭 -------- |
| ------------------ 各9 5公克 |
| 蝦米 ------------- 3 7 公克 |

1 **1**料洗淨加水浸泡1 2 小時後，瀝乾水分，另外加3 杯水，用果汁機打成米漿。
2 蝦米洗淨切末，廣式香腸切0．5公分小丁，紅蔥頭切細末備用。
3 鍋熱入油4 大匙燒熱，入白蘿蔔絲炒軟備用。
4 另鍋熱入油3 大匙，入**2**料炒香，再入**3**料及炒軟的白蘿蔔絲拌勻，熄火後倒入米漿拌勻，再倒入舖好玻璃紙的容器中，入蒸鍋大火蒸1 小時即可。

1200g.(2³/₅lb.) -- shredded turnip

1 sheet-cellophane paper

1
- •480g.(17oz.) long grain rice
- •120g.(4¼oz.) short grain rice

2
- •95g.(3³/₁₀oz.) each Cantonese sausage, red shallots
- •37g.(1³/₁₀oz.) dried baby shrimp

3
- •1T.salt
- •1t.pepper

1 Rinse **1**, soak in water for 12 hours, drain. Add 3C. water, puree in a blender.
2 Wash dried shrimp clean and mince. Cut sausage into 0.5 cm (⅕") small cubes. Mince shallots.
3 Heat the wok, add 4T. oil and heat, stir fry turnip until softened.
4 Heat another wok, add 3T. oil, stir fry **2** until fragrant. Add **3** and softened turnip, mix well. Turn off heat, stir in rice puree in evenly. Pour into cellophane-lined container, steam over high heat for 1 hour. Remove and allow to cool. Cut into thick serving slices, fry with a little oil in a pan until golden.

油蔥糕 • *Pork and Shallot Rice Cake*

在來米、蓬萊米 各300公克　　油蔥酥 ------------------------ ½杯
地瓜粉、絞肉 --- 各150公克　　玻璃紙 ------------------------ 1張
鹽 ------------------------ 1大匙

1[醬油 ------------------ 2小匙
　 胡椒粉 、味精 -- 各½小匙

1 在來米、蓬萊米洗淨泡水約3小時，瀝乾加水2杯與地瓜粉、鹽用果汁機打成米漿後，入6杯沸水拌勻，即為米漿。
2 鍋熱入油2大匙燒熱，入油蔥酥與絞肉炒熟，續入 **1** 料拌勻即為肉餡。
3 取 ⅔ 肉餡入米漿中拌勻，倒入鋪好玻璃紙的蒸籠中，再將剩餘之肉餡鋪於米漿上，入鍋大火蒸50分鐘即可。

300g.(10½oz.) each - long grain rice, short grain rice
150g.(5⅓oz.) each - sweet potato flour, ground pork

1T. ----------------------- salt
½C. ---- fried shallot flakes
1 sheet - cellophane paper

1[• 2t.soy sauce
　 • ½t.pepper

1 Rinse both types of rice and soak in water for 3 hours, drain. Mix 2C. water, sweet potato flour,and salt, together with rice, puree in a blender. Pour in 6C. hot water and mix well.
2 Heat the wok, add 2T. oil and heat; stir fry shallot flakes and ground pork until done. Add **1** then mix well. This is the filling.
3 Mix ⅔ of filling into rice puree evenly, pour in cellophane-lined steamer. Spread the rest of filling on top. Steam over high heat for 50 minutes.

九層糕 • *Nine-layered Cake*

在來米 ------------- 200公克	太白粉 -------------------- 3大匙	200g.(7oz.)long grain rice	3T. ------------- corn starch
1 ┌ 水 ----------------- 1杯 ├ 二砂紅糖 ------------- ³⁄₄杯 └ 紅糖 ------------- 1⅓大匙	**2** ┌ 水 ----------------- 1杯 └ 糖 ----------------- ³⁄₄杯	**1** ┌ •1C.water ├ •³⁄₄C. brown sugar └ •1⅓T.dark brown 　 sugar	**2** ┌ •1C.water └ •³⁄₄C.sugar

1 米洗淨泡水3小時後瀝乾,加2杯水打成米漿,續入太白粉拌勻並分成2等份。

2 **1**料拌勻至糖溶解入1份米漿為赤漿,**2**料拌勻至糖溶解再入另1份米漿為白漿。

3 蒸盤抹少許油,先入鍋蒸熱,倒入半杯赤漿蒸7分鐘後(圖1),再入半杯白漿蒸7分鐘(圖2),如此重複至米漿倒完,最後再蒸20分鐘,取出後待涼切塊即可。

■ 雙味九層糕:將 **2** 料改為鹽2小匙及水1杯,其餘材料及做法與九層糕相同。

1 Rinse rice and soak in water for 3 hours, drain. Add 2C. water, puree in a blender, mix in corn starch. Divide into 2 equal portions.

2 Mix **1** well until sugar has dissoved, add one portion of rice puree. This will be the brown rice puree. Mix **2** well until sugar dissolved, add the other portion of puree. This will be the white rice puree.

3 Grease a steam tray, put in a steamer and steam until the tray is very hot. Pour in half cup of brown rice puree and steam for 7 minutes (illus. 1). Then add half cup of white rice puree and steam for 7 minutes (illus. 2). Repeat the process until both are finished. At last, steam for 20 more minutes. Remove and allow to cool. Cut into serving slices.

■ Double-flavored Nine-layered Cake: Replaced **2** with 2t. salt and 1C. water. The rest of materials and methods are the same as above.

1

2

倫敎糕 • *Run Jiau Rice Cake*

在來米 -------------- 600公克　　玻璃紙 --------------------- 1 張
蒸盤 ------------------------- 1 個

1 ⎡ 水 ----------------------- 3 杯
　　⎣ 糖 ----------------------- 2 杯

2 ⎡ 溫水 ----------------- 2 大匙
　　⎣ 酵母 ------------------- ½ 大匙

1 米泡水 3 小時後瀝乾，加 **1** 料打成米漿，用小火煮至輕微糊狀，煮時須不停攪拌，以免結塊或燒焦，然後過濾待涼。

2 **2** 料攪拌均勻後，靜置 1 0 分鐘，即為酵母水，再加入已涼之米漿發酵至表面起很多氣泡（約 6 ～ 8 小時），即倒入已舖好玻璃紙的蒸盤內入鍋大火蒸 3 5 分鐘至熟即可。

600g.(1⅓lb.) --- long grain rice

1 ----------------- steam tray
1 sheet - cellophane paper

1 ⎡ •3C.water
　　⎣ •2C.sugar

2 ⎡ •2T.warm water
　　⎣ •½T.active dry yeast

1 Soak rice in water for 3 hours and drain. Add **1** and puree in a blender. Boil over low heat until thick, stir constantly during boiling to avoid burning or lumps. Run through a sieve and allow to cool.

2 Mix **2** well and let it stand for 10 minutes, then add rice puree, mix well and let it stand until bubbly on the surface (about 6 to 8 hours). Pour in cellophane-lined steam tray in a steamer and steam over high heat for 35 minutes, and serve.

梗仔糕 • *Soda Rice Cake*

1 ⎡ 在來米、蓬萊米 ----------
　　⎢ ---------------- 各 3 0 0 公克
　　⎢ 樹薯粉 -------- 2 0 0 公克
　　⎣ 水 ----------------------- 2 杯

2 ⎡ 鹼粉 ----------------- 6 公克
　　⎣ 食用黃色 5 號 ------ ⅛ 小匙

1 在來米及蓬萊米均洗淨泡水 3 小時，瀝乾備用。

2 **1** 料磨成米漿，加入 **2** 料拌勻，再以熱開水 6 杯拌成糊狀，倒入已抹好油的蒸盤中入鍋大火蒸 4 0 分鐘，待涼切塊沾蜂蜜或糖漿吃即可。

1 ⎡ •300g.(10½oz.) each long grain rice, short grain rice
　　⎢ •200g.(7oz.) tapioca
　　⎣ •2C.water

2 ⎡ •6g.(⅕oz.)baking soda
　　⎣ •⅛t.yellow food coloring

1 Rinse both types of rice and soak in water for 3 hours, drain.

2 Puree **1** in a blender, add **2** and mix well. Pour in 6C. hot water and mix into a paste. Pour into a greased tray in a steamer, steam over high heat for 40 minutes. Remove and allow to cool. Serve with syrup or honey.

椰子涼糕 •*Coconut Rice Cake*

椰子粉 -------------- １００公克

❶　糯米粉 -------- １５０公克
　　澄粉 ------------- ５０公克

❷　椰漿 ------------------ １杯
　　細糖、水 ----------- 各½杯
　　鮮奶 ------------------- ¼杯
　　油 -------------------- ３大匙

1 **❶**料過篩，**❷**料煮至完全溶解，再入 **❶** 料煮成糊狀，倒入蒸盤中入鍋大火蒸１０分鐘，取出待涼切塊即為涼糕。
2 椰子粉先入烤箱烤成金黃色，再取涼糕沾上椰子粉即可。

100g.(3½oz.) -- desiccated coconut

❶　•150g.(5⅓oz.) glutinous rice flour
　　•50g.(1¾oz.) wheat starch

❷　•1C.coconut cream
　　•½C.each sugar, water
　　•¼C.milk
　　•3T.oil

1 Sift **❶**. Boil **❷** until dissolved, mix in **❶** and simmer until thickened. Pour into tray in a steamer, steam over high heat for 10 minutes.　Remove and allow to cool. Cut into serving pieces.
2 Roast coconut in the oven until golden. Sprinkle on the cake　and serve.

甜米糍 • *Chilled Coconut Ball*

椰子粉 -------------- １００公克

❶　糯米粉 -------- ２００公克
　　澄粉 ------------- ８０公克

❷　水 ---------------------- １¾杯
　　細糖 -------------------- ¾杯
　　花生油、奶水 -- 各４大匙

1 **❶**料過篩，**❷**料拌勻至糖溶解，再加入過篩的 **❶** 料拌勻，入鍋大火蒸３５分鐘，取出待完全涼透放入冰箱冰涼，再取出揉勻，分成適當大小之小糰並沾椰子粉即可食用。

100g.(3½oz.) -- desiccated coconut

❶　•200g.(7oz.) glutinous rice flour
　　•80g.(2⅘oz.) wheat starch

❷　•1¾C.water
　　•¾C.sugar
　　•4T.each oil, evaporated milk

1 Sift **❶**. Mix **❷** until sugar has dissolved, and mix with **❶** well. Steam over high heat for 35 minutes. Remove and allow to cool, then chill in refrigerator. Knead into serving sized balls, roll in coconut, and serve.

•Pork Rice Cake

鹹年糕 • *Pork Rice Cake*

圓糯米	----------------	5 2 5公克
在來米	----------------	2 2 5公克
里肌肉	----------------	1 5 0公克
蝦米	----------------	4 0公克
香菇	----------------	1 0公克
紅蔥頭末	----------------	3 大匙
中空竹管	----------------	4 個
玻璃紙	----------------	¼張

1
- 鹽 ---------------- 2小匙
- 胡椒粉、味精 -- 各1小匙

1 圓糯米、在來米混合洗淨，加水浸泡3小時，製成粿粉糰。

2 香菇、蝦米泡軟洗淨切丁，里肌肉切丁。鍋熱入油4大匙燒熱，入紅蔥頭炒香，續入蝦米、香菇、里肌肉炒熟，再入 **1** 料拌炒均勻備用。

3 將粿粉糰搓碎（圖1），取5 0公克入鍋蒸熟（或煮熟），再加入炒好的餡及剩下之粿粉糰揉均勻（圖2）即為粿糰。

4 備一蒸籠，蒸籠四周插入竹管，舖上玻璃紙，再入粿糰，蓋上蒸籠蓋，入鍋蒸3小時，待筷子插入不黏時即可，最後將竹管拿開待涼，凝固後即可切食。

525g.(18½oz.)	short grain glutinous rice
225g.(8oz.)	long grain rice
150g.(5⅓oz.)	pork fillet
40g.(1⅖oz.)	dried baby shrimp
10g.(⅓oz.)	dried black mushrooms
3T.	minced red shallot
4	bamboo tubes
¼ sheet	cellophane paper

1
- 2t.salt
- 1t.pepper

1 Rinse and mix both types of rice, soak in water for 3 hours and make into fine flour dough (see P.10).

2 Soften mushrooms and shrimp in warm water, chop. Dice pork. Heat the wok, add 4T. oil and heat; stir fry shallots until fragrant. Add shrimp, mushrooms, and pork, fry until done. Season with **1**, and mix well. This is the filling.

3 Break rice flour dough into fine crumbs (illus. 1), steam 50g.(1¾oz.) until cooked. Mix steamed dough, the filling, and the rest of rice flour dough, mix well (illus. 2).

4 Place bamboo tubes around the edge of a steamer, line the bottom with cellophane paper. Put the dough on the paper, cover with lid and steam for 3 hours, or until chopstick comes out clean. Remove the bamboo tubes and allow to cool. When set, cut into serving pieces and serve.

1

2

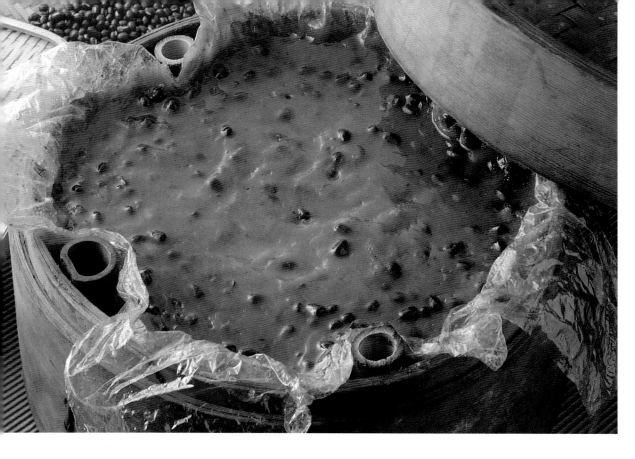

紅豆年糕 • *Red Bean Rice Cake*

圓糯米 -------------- 900公克	中空竹管 -------------------- 4個	900g.(2lb.) ---- short grain glutinous rice	5¼C. ------- golden brown sugar
紅豆 ----------------- 300公克	玻璃紙 ----------------------- 1張	300g.(10½oz.) - red beans	4 ------------ bamboo tubes
二砂紅糖 ------------------ 5¼杯			1 sheet - cellophane paper

1 紅豆洗淨，加水5杯浸泡3小時，入鍋小火煮至紅豆軟而不裂開且汁快收乾（約1小時），再加1½杯糖煮化即成紅豆餡。

2 圓糯米洗淨，加水浸泡3小時製成粿粉糰，再將粿粉糰搓碎，加糖3¾杯搓揉至糖溶化，再入紅豆餡拌勻。

3 備一蒸籠，蒸籠四周插入竹管（圖1），舖上玻璃紙（圖2），再將糯米漿倒入，蓋上蒸籠蓋，入鍋大火蒸3小時，至筷子插入不黏時，再將竹管拿開吹涼，並待凝固後即可。

1 Wash red beans and soak in 5C. water for 3 hours. Boil over low heat until red beans are tender, but have not opened, and with only a little soup left (about 1 hour). Add 1½C. sugar to form a paste.

2 Rinse rice and soak in water for 3 hours, make into rice flour dough, break into fine crumbs. Mix with 3¾C. sugar and knead until sugar is completely dissolved. Mix well with red bean paste.

3 Place bamboo tubes around the edge of a steamer (illus. 1), line the bottom with cellophane paper (illus. 2). Pour in the batter, cover with lid. Steam over high heat for 3 hours, or until chopstick comes out clean when poked. Remove bamboo tubes and allow to cool. When set, cut into serving pieces.

1

2

寧波年糕 •*Nin Po Rice Cake*

蓬萊米 -------------- ６００公克

1 蓬萊米洗淨加水浸泡製成粿粉糰，再將粿粉糰用篩子篩細。
2 備一蒸籠，內放蒸籠布，將篩過的粉均勻灑入（圖１），另在蒸籠口罩上一層濕布（圖２）。
3 將蒸籠入鍋，大火蒸３０分鐘後，掀去蒸籠布，用長筷略翻粉末，再將蒸籠布打濕罩上，續蒸１５分鐘，取下布巾，倒入盆中。
4 用一根木杵或擀麵棍樁打糕糰百來下，取出趁熱用手大力搓揉，使其均勻緊實。
5 將糕糰分成１２個，再搓成直徑２．５公分、長１０公分的圓條，稍加壓扁即可。
■ 吃寧波年糕時可切片與肉絲、青菜同炒，或入高湯中煮成年糕湯。

600g.(1⅓lb.) --------- short grain rice

1 Make rice into rice flour dough (see P. 10). Sift dough in a sieve to make fine rice flour.
2 Place a cloth in a steamer, sprinkle sifted rice flour on it (illus. 1). Cover the steamer with a wet cloth (illus. 2).
3 Steam over high heat for 30 minutes, remove the covering cloth; stir the flour slightly with long chopsticks. Wet the covering cloth, and cover again, continue to steam for another 15 minutes. Pour into a shallow container.
4 Beat the dough with a wooden pestle or a rolling pin for a hundred times. While warm, knead the dough hard to make stiff.
5 Divide the dough into 12 equal portions, knead them into 2.5 cm x 10 cm (1 " x 4") round strips; press to flatten. Cut into slanted pieces. Can be used as fried rice cake or soup rice cake.

1

2

甜年糕 • *Sweet Rice Cake*

圓糯米 -------------- ９００公克　　中空竹管 -------------------- 4 個
二砂紅糖 ----------------- 1 ¾杯　　玻璃紙 ----------------------- 1 張

1 圓糯米先做成粿粉糰再搓碎，加入二砂紅糖，一起搓揉至糖溶化，即為糯米漿。
2 備一蒸籠，蒸籠四周先插入竹管，再鋪上玻璃紙，再將糯米漿倒入，蓋上蒸籠蓋，入鍋大火蒸約 3 小時，待筷子插入不黏時即可。

900g.(2lb.) ---- short grain　4 ------------ bamboo tubes
glutinous rice　　　　　　　1 sheet - cellophane paper
1¾C. ------- golden brown
sugar

1 Make rice dough with glutinous rice (see P. 10), break the dough to fine crumbs, mix with sugar, knead until sugar is dissolved.
2 Place bamboo tubes along the inner edge of the steamer. Line the bottom of the steamer with cellophane paper (see p.72), pour in rice batter; cover and steam over high heat for 3 hours. Poke a chopstick through the rice cake, it is done when the chopstick comes out clean.

蘇式桂花年糕 • *Soo Chow Osmanthus New Year Cake*

糯米粉 -------------- ３４０公克　　糖 ---------------------------- 1 ⅕杯
熱開水 --------------------- 1 ½杯　　桂花醬 --------------------- 1 大匙

1 糯米粉過篩，加熱開水揉拌均勻，分兩糰，放入墊有濕蒸籠布的蒸籠中，入鍋大火蒸３０分鐘，取出倒入盆中加糖及桂花醬攪拌均勻後，用木杵或擀麵棍大力樁攪成糰再整型即可。

340g.(12oz.) ---- glutinous　1⅕C. ------------------ sugar
rice flour　　　　　　　　1T. sweet osmanthus jam
1½C. ------------- hot water

1 Sift rice flour, add hot water, knead well. Divide dough into two portions. Place in a wet cheese cloth lined steamer, steam over high heat for 30 minutes, remove and place in a shallow pan. Mix in sugar and osmanthus jam, blend well, with a wooden pestle or rolling pin pound into two smooth pieces of dough. Re-shape.

紅豆鬆糕 • *Red Bean Sand Cake*

紅豆 -------------------- 7 5 公克　　　糖 ----------------------------- 3/8杯

1[在來米粉 ----- 2 2 5 公克　　**2**[糖、水 ---------------- 各1/2杯
　　糯米粉 ----------- 7 5 公克

1 紅豆洗淨，泡水 6 小時，再放入電鍋蒸熟（約 1 小時），取出倒去湯汁，加入糖拌勻放涼備用。

2 **1**料混合均勻過篩，再將**2**料溶解均勻，倒入**1**料中，搓揉成細粉狀，用篩子再過篩一次即為米粉。

3 白紙剪一圓形，墊於蒸籠裡，先舖半量米粉，再灑上紅豆，最上面再灑上半量米粉，入鍋大火蒸 3 0 分鐘，取出切塊即可。

75g.(2²/₃oz.) ---- red beans　　³/₈C. --------------------sugar

1[• 225g.(8oz.) long　　**2**[• 1/2C. each sugar,
　　grain rice flour　　　　　　　water
　　• 75g.(2²/₃oz.)
　　glutinous rice flour

1 Wash red beans, soak in water for 6 hours, cook in rice cooker until done (about 1 hour). Remove, drain, add sugar, mix well and allow to cool.

2 Mix **1** well and sift. Melt **2** and stir well, pour into **1**. Knead into fine powder, sift again.

3 Line the steamer with a sheet of round white paper, spread one layer with half of the rice powder, sprinkle on one layer of red beans, cover with the other half of the rice powder. Steam over high heat for 30 minutes. Cut into serving pieces and serve.

豆沙糕餅 • *Stuffed Red Bean Ball*

豆沙 ------------------ 3 0 0 公克　　**1**[糯米粉 -------- 3 0 0 公克
粽葉 -------------------------- 5 張　　　　澄粉 ------------- 6 0 公克

1 取豆沙 1 6 0 公克，分成每個 8 公克共 2 0 個豆沙餡，粽葉洗淨剪成正方形 2 0 張備用。

2 **1**料過篩入沸水 1 杯拌勻，續入冷水 1/3 杯及豆沙 1 4 0 公克揉勻，搓成長條狀，分成 2 0 等份，每份搓成圓球，再壓成圓皮包入豆沙餡，收口包住揉圓，置於抹過油的粽葉上，入鍋大火蒸 5 分鐘至熟即可。

300g.(10¹/₂oz.) --red bean paste
5 ---broad bamboo leaves

1[• 300g.(10¹/₂oz.)
　　glutinous rice flour
　　• 60g.(2¹/₁₀oz.) wheat
　　starch

1 Divide 160g.(5¹/₄oz.) red bean paste into 20 equal fillings with 20g.(²/₃oz.) each. Wash bamboo leaves and cut into 20 squares.

2 Sift **1** and add 1C. hot water, mix well, then mix in ¹/₃C. cold water and 140g.(5oz.) red bean paste, knead well and roll into a long strip. Divide the strip into 20 equal portions, knead each portion into a ball and press into a fat round circle. To be used as wrapper. Wrap a red bean paste filling in the center, roll into a ball. Makes 20. Place each ball on one greased bamboo square, steam over high heat until done.

蕉油軟糕 • *Banana Flavored Cake*

豆沙 ----------------- 220公克	糖粉 ------------------------¼杯
糯米粉 -------------- 200公克	太白粉 --------------------- 1 大匙

❶ ⌈ 油 -------------------- 1 大匙
　　⌊ 香蕉油 ------------- 1 小匙

1 糯米粉置盆內，入開水 ½ 杯先拌勻，再加冷水 ⅓ 杯揉拌均勻成糰，入鍋大火蒸 2 0 分鐘，即為熟糯米糰。

2 熟糯米糰待涼，加 **❶** 料揉至光滑，再分割成每個 2 0 公克之小塊。

3 豆沙分成每份 1 0 公克，每個糯米糰包入 1 份豆沙，若會黏手，可沾少許太白粉，再捏成橢圓型或隨自己喜愛捏成各種造型即可 。

220g.(7³/₄oz.) --- red bean paste	¼C. -------------- powdered sugar
200g.(7oz.) ----- glutinous rice flour	1T. ------------- corn starch

❶ ⌈ • 1T.oil
　　⌊ • 1t.banana essence

1 Place rice flour in a shallow plate, mix well with ½C. hot water, then mix well with ⅓C. cold water, knead into a dough. Steam over high heat for 20 minutes.

2 Allow rice dough to cool, then knead with **❶** until shiny and smooth. Divide into small pieces, 20g.(²/₃ oz.) each.

3 Divide red bean paste into small portions, 10g.(¹/₃oz.) each. Wrap rice dough around a red bean paste. Dust with corn starch if needed to avoid sticking to fingers. Roll into oblong shape or any other desired shapes.

麻薯 • *Peanut Mochi*

| 圓糯米 -------------- ３００公克 | 細糖 --------------------- ２⅔大匙 |
| 豆沙 ---------------- ２００公克 | 雪白油 ------------------- ２小匙 |

1⎡ 花生粉 ------------- ５大匙
　⎣ 細糖 ----------------- ２大匙

1 米洗淨，加水浸泡並製成粿粉糰、捏碎，入已鋪好布之蒸籠內
　　（圖１），大火蒸３０分鐘，取出趁熱倒入盆中，加入細糖，用
　　木杵或擀麵棍用力椿攪（圖２）糕糰，至糖溶化十分均勻，即為
　　粿糰。
2 手上沾雪白油，抓起一把糕糰，用虎口擠成一塊（約１５公克）
　　（圖３），直接沾上拌勻的 **1** 料，或是粿糰中間包入豆沙餡５
　　公克，外面再沾上 **1** 料均可。

| 300g.(10½oz.) -------short grain glutinous rice 20g.(7oz.) red bean paste | 2⅔T. ---------------------- sugar 2t. -------------- shortening |

1⎡ •5T.peanut powder
　⎣ •2T.sugar

1 Rinse rice, soak in water and make into rice flour dough then break into fine crumbs. Place into cloth lined steamer (illus. 1), steam over high heat for 30 minutes. Pour into a shallow plate while still warm. Mix in sugar, beat with a wooden pestle or rolling pin (illus. 2) until sugar has melted evenly.
2 Grease hands with shortening, squeeze dough into small (about 15g./ ½oz. each) pieces (illus. 3). Either roll in well- mixed **1** , or wrap around 5g.(⅙oz.) red bean paste filling in and roll in **1** .

1

2

3

荸薺餅 • *Water Chestnut Pastry*

荸薺 ----------------- 750公克	在來米粉 -------------- 60公克	750g.(1³/₅lb.) --------water chestnuts	60g.(2¹/₁₀oz.) ---long grain rice flour
豆沙 ----------------- 120公克		120g.(4¹/₄oz.) ----red bean paste	

1 ┌ 水 ----------------------- ½杯
  └ 糖 -------------------- 3大匙

2 ┌ 水 --------------------- 1大匙
  └ 太白粉 -------------- ½大匙

1 荸薺去皮洗淨，用磨泥器磨成泥，再將荸薺汁擠出備用，荸薺渣則加在來米粉拌勻。

2 豆沙分成12份，荸薺渣亦分成12份，每份荸薺渣按壓成扁平狀，中間包入豆沙，收口揉圓，即成荸薺粉糰。

3 鍋熱入油6杯燒至七分熱（160℃），入荸薺粉糰炸至金黃色，撈起瀝油，並將荸薺糰用鏟子按扁，即成荸薺餅。

4 取荸薺汁½杯加 **1** 料入鍋煮開，再入 **2** 料芶芡即為荸薺糖汁，食時淋在荸薺餅上即可。

1 ┌ •½C.water
  └ •3T.sugar

2 ┌ •1T.water
  └ •½T.corn starch

1 Skin water chestnuts and wash, mash into paste, drain the juice into a small container for later use. Mix water chestnut paste with rice flour well.

2 Divide red bean paste and water chestnut mixture into 12 equal portions. Press each portion of water chestnut mixture into a round flat wrapper, place one portion of red bean paste in the center. Seal the opening and roll into a ball. Makes 12.

3 Heat the wok, add 6C. oil and heat to 160℃ (320°F), deep fry water chestnut balls until golden. Lift out and drain. Flatten the balls slightly with a spatula.

4 Add ½C. water to chestnut juice and **1**, bring to a boil. Thicken with **2**, and pour over pastries and serve.

元宵 • *Lantern Festival Mochi Ball*

糯米粉 ------------- 150公克	❶	糖粉 -------------- 3⅓大匙 黑芝麻粉 --------- 2⅔大匙 豬油 -------------- 2½大匙 雪白油 ------------- 1大匙

1 將❶料拌勻成餡，放入冰箱冷凍30分鐘，取出搓成每個約10公克圓球，再入冰箱冷凍30分鐘備用。

2 備一盆清水，將冰凍的餡取出放在漏勺上，先過水5秒（圖1），立即放入鋪有糯米粉之圓盆中，以順時鐘方向搖動（圖2），使餡球沾上糯米粉。

3 餡球沾裹一層粉後，再度過水，撈起繼續沾裹第二層粉，如此相同方式共沾八次即成生元宵。

4 5杯水煮開入生元宵待沸騰後改小火煮15分鐘至元宵浮起即可。

■ 元宵的內餡中，黑芝麻粉可以花生粉取代。

150g.(5⅓oz.) --- glutinous rice flour	❶	• 3⅓T.powdered sugar • 2⅔T.black sesame powder • 2½T.lard • 1T.shortening

1 Mix ❶ well for the filling, chill in refrigerator for 30 minutes. Knead into balls, 10g.(⅓oz.) each, chill again for 30 minutes.

2 Place chilled filling balls on a sieve ladle and lower into a large bowl of cold water for 5 seconds (illus. 1). Immediately roll the filling balls, clockwise, on a round rice flour tray (illus. 2). The filling balls should be coated completely with rice flour.

3 Lower the coated balls in the water again, roll on the rice flour tray until completely coated for the second time. Repeat the process until the filling balls are coated 8 times.

4 Bring 5C. water to a boil, drop in rice balls, and simmer over low heat for 15 minutes or until the rice balls float on top.

■ Peanut powder may be used, instead of black sesame powder as the filling.

1

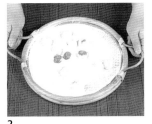

2

草仔粿 • *Tsao Ah Guey*

圓糯米 -------------- ６００公克
乾眉殼草 ------------ ４０公克
美人蕉葉或粽葉 -------- １０張
粿模 ------------------ １個

1
糖 ------------------ ５大匙
水 ------------------ ２杯

2
絞肉 ----------- １５０公克
乾蘿蔔絲 -------- ７０公克
蝦米 ------------ ２０公克
香菇 ------------ １５公克

3
水 ---------------------¼杯
醬油、糖 -------- 各１大匙
鹽 ----------------- １½小匙
胡椒粉 -------------- ¾小匙

4
水 ---------------- ６大匙
太白粉 ------------ ２小匙

1 圓糯米洗淨，製成粿粉糰，美人蕉葉洗淨備用。
2 乾眉殼草（圖１）泡水洗淨，入開水川燙後待涼，將粗枝挑掉、擠乾水分，切細末入 **1** 料煮至汁收乾，趁熱倒入捻碎的粿粉糰中，揉拌均勻即為粿糰。
3 乾蘿蔔絲泡水洗淨切段，蝦米、香菇泡軟洗淨切細丁，鍋熱入油４大匙燒熱，入 **2** 料炒熟，再入 **3** 料炒拌均勻，並入 **4** 料芶芡待涼，即為肉餡。
4 將粿糰分成１０份，中間填入肉餡５０公克，收口包住揉圓。
5 粿模刷上一層油（圖２），把粉糰壓入模中（圖３），覆上一張抹過油的美人蕉葉，將粉糰倒扣出來（圖４），多餘的葉緣修齊後，入鍋大火蒸１０分鐘即可。

600g.(1⅓lb.) ---------------------- short grain glutinous rice
40g.(1⅖oz.) ------------------------------------ dried cudweed
10 ------------------------ banana leaves or bamboo leaves
1 --- tsao ah guey mold

1
• 5T.sugar
• 2C.water

2
• 150g.(5⅓oz.) minced pork
• 70g.(2½oz.) shredded dried turnip
• 20g.(⅔oz.) dried baby shrimp
• 15g.(½oz.) dried black mushrooms

3
• ¼C.water
• 1T.each soy sauce, sugar
• 1½t.salt
• ¾t.pepper

4
• 6T.water
• 2t.corn starch

1 Rinse rice, and make into rice flour dough. Wash leaves.
2 Soak cudweed (illus. 1) and parboil in boiling water, allow to cool. Discard tough branches, squeeze out excess water and mince. Boil minced cudweed with **1** until liquid is reduced. While warm, mix in crumbled rice flour dough. Knead well.
3 Soak shredded turnip, rinse and cut into sections. Soften mushrooms and shrimp in warm water, rinse and dice. Heat the wok, add 4T. oil and heat; stir fry **2** until done. Season with **3** and mix well. Thicken with **4**. This will be the filling.
4 Divide the dough into 10 equal portions, each wrap in 50g.(1¾oz.) of filling, roll to seal the opening tightly. Makes 10.
5 Grease the mold (illus. 2), press in one portion of stuffed dough (illus. 3), cover with a greased leaf. Invert the dough (illus. 4), trim off excess leaf. Steam over high heat for 10 minutes and serve.

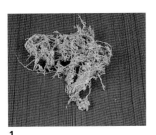
1

2

3

4

紅龜粿 • *Festive Red Turtle Cake*

圓糯米 ------------- 600公克	龜形粿模 -------------------- 1個	600g.(1⅓lb.) --short grain glutinous rice	1 ------turtle-shaped mold
豆沙 ------------- 400公克	蕉葉或粽葉 ------------- 10張	400g.(14oz.) ----red bean paste	10 -----------banana leaves or bamboo leaves

1［ 水 ------------------- 1小匙
　　食用紅色6號 ------ ⅛小匙

1［ •1t.water
　　•⅛t.red food coloring

1 圓糯米洗淨，加水浸泡，製成粿粉糰，蕉葉洗淨。

2 取粿粉糰100公克，入開水中煮10分鐘，見糕糰浮起，撈起瀝乾，和入剩餘粿粉糰，再加 **1** 料，揉拌均勻。

3 豆沙分成10份，粿粉糰亦分成10份，揉成圓粿糰，中間包入豆沙，收口捏緊揉圓。

4 粿模先刷上油，再把粉糰慢慢按壓入模子（圖1），上面覆上一張抹過油的蕉葉，將粉糰倒扣出來（圖2），多餘的葉緣修齊，入鍋大火蒸7分鐘即可。

■ 粿的內餡，可以綠豆沙或花生粉取代。

1 Rinse rice, soak in water and make into rice flour dough. Wash leaves.

2 Boil 100g.(3½oz.) of rice flour dough in boiling water for 10 minutes. When floats, lift the dough out and drain. Mix boiled dough with the rest of the dough, and add **1**. Knead well.

3 Divide red bean paste and the rice dough into 10 equal portions. Knead each dough into a round piece, place the red bean paste filling in the center, roll up the opening tightly. Makes 10.

4 Grease the mold, press in cake slowly (illus. 1). Cover with a sheet of greased leaf. Invert the dough (illus. 2), trim off excess leaf. Steam over high heat for 7 minutes.

■ This cake is served for celebrations.

■ Mung bean paste or sweet peanut powder may be substituted for red bean paste as filling.

1

2

芋粿巧 • *Pork and Taro Cake*

芋頭（淨重）------ 6 0 0公克		粽葉 ---------------------- 1 0張	
1	蓬萊米 ----- 1 0 5 0公克 圓糯米 -------- 3 0 0公克	**3**	鹽 -------------------- 2 小匙 胡椒粉、糖 ----- 各 1 小匙
2	里肌肉 -------- 3 0 0公克 紅蔥頭 ----------- 6 0公克 蝦米 ------------- 3 0公克		

1 **1** 料洗淨加水浸泡，製成粿粉糰，再將粿粉糰搓碎備用。
2 芋頭刨絲，**2** 料全部切小丁。
3 鍋熱入油4大匙燒熱，炒香 **2** 料，再入 **3** 料拌炒均勻後，盛起，倒入搓碎粿粉糰中，再加入芋頭絲，將全部材料揉均勻（圖1），搓成長條狀，分成2 2個（每個1 0 0公克）。
4 取每個粿糰，用手稍搓圓，再壓成半月型（圖2），底下墊抹油粽葉，入鍋大火蒸3 0分鐘即可。

600g.(1⅓lb.) ----taros (net weight)		10 - broad bamboo leaves	
1	•1050g.(2³/₁₀lb.) short grain rice •300g.(10½oz.) short grain glutinous rice	**2**	•300g.(10½oz.) pork fillet •60g.(2¹/₁₀oz.) red shallots •30g.(1oz.) dried baby shrimp
3	•2t.salt •1t.each sugar, pepper		

1 Rinse **1** and soak in water. Form into rice flour dough (see p. 10), break the dough into fine crumbs.
2 Shred taros. Dice all **2**.
3 Heat the wok, add 4T. oil and heat; stir fry **2** until fragrant, season with **3**, remove. Mix in rice dough crumbs and add shredded taros(illus. 1). Knead evenly and roll into long strips. Divide into 22 equal portions (about 100g. or 3½oz.).
4 Roll each portion into a ball, press into crescent shape (illus. 2). Place on greased bamboo leaves, steam over high heat for 30 minutes.

1

2

米苔目 • *Mi Tai Ma*

在來米 -------------- ６００公克	太白粉 --------------------- ２大匙	

1 在來米洗淨泡水３小時瀝乾水分，再加水３杯打成米漿，取三分之二壓乾成粿粉糰，再用手捻碎。

2 將剩下的米漿加入冷水４杯稀釋，倒入鍋中以小火煮至黏稠狀（約５分鐘），再入捻碎的粿粉糰及太白粉一起搓揉，成為粿粉糰。

3 半鍋水煮開，將米苔目板橫架在鍋上，再把揉好的粿粉糰放在米苔目板上用均等的力量來回搓揉，使米苔目從篩孔掉入鍋中（圖１），見米苔目浮出水面，用漏勺盛起，過一次冷水即可。

600g.(1⅓lb.) ---Indica rice	2T. -------------- corn starch

1 Rinse rice and soak in water for 3 hours, drain. Puree rice with 3C. water. Press two third of rice puree dry, and break it into fine crumbs by hand.

2 Dilute the remaining one third of rice puree with 4C. cold water, pour into a pot and simmer over low heat until thickened (about 5 minutes). Knead into rice crumbs and corn starch until doughy.

3 Bring half pot of water to a boil, place Mi Tai Ma board over the pot widthwise. Knead the rice dough back and forth over the board with equal strength, shaving the dough into shreds. The shaved dough will drop into the boiling water through the holes on the board (illus. 1). This dough shreds are called Mi Tai Ma. When the shreaded dough or Mi Tai Ma floats on top of the water, lift out with a sieve ladle, rinse once under cold water. Mi Tai Ma can be used in soups.

1

肉燥米苔目 • *Mi Tai Ma Meat Sauce*

米苔目 -------------- 900公克	紅蔥頭 ---------------- 60公克	900g.(2lb.) ----- Mi Tai Ma	60g.(2¹/₁₀oz.) -- red shallots
絞肉 ----------------- 300公克	韭菜 ------------------- 20公克	300g.(10½oz.) ---- ground pork	20g.(2/3 oz.) -------- chives
綠豆芽 -------------- 150公克	蝦米末 ---------------- 5大匙	150g.(5¹/₃oz.) - mung bean sprouts	5T. ---- minced dried baby shrimp

1 醬油、酒 --------- 各2大匙

2 ⎡ 高湯 ------------------ 5杯
   ⎢ 醬油 ------------------ 1大匙
   ⎢ 鹽、味精、胡椒粉 --------
   ⎣ ------------------ 各½小匙

1 [•2T.each soy sauce, cooking wine

2 ⎡ •5C.stock
   ⎢ •1T.soy sauce
   ⎣ •½t.each salt, pepper

1 紅蔥頭洗淨切片，韭菜切3公分長段備用。
2 鍋熱入油2大匙燒熱，入紅蔥頭及蝦米爆香，再入絞肉炒熟後，以 **1** 料調味並燜煮5分鐘即為肉燥。
3 **2** 料煮開入韭菜及綠豆芽煮開即為湯汁。
4 米苔目入開水中川燙，撈起置於碗內，入湯汁並淋上肉燥即可。

1 Wash shallots and slice. Cut chives into 3 cm (1⅕") long sections.
2 Heat the wok, add 2T. oil and heat; stir fry shallots and shrimp until fragrant. Stir in pork and fry until cooked. Season with **1** and simmer for 5 minutes for the meat sauce.
3 Bring **2** to a boil, add chives and mung bean sprouts.
4 Parboil Mi Tai Ma in boiling water, drain. Place in individual serving bowls, pour soup over, spoon meat sauce on top, and serve.

芋頭米粉 • *Taro Soup Rice Noodles*

粗米粉（濕）------ 4 5 0公克	蒜末 --------------------- 2 大匙		
芋頭（淨重）------ 4 0 0公克	高湯 ----------------------- 1 2杯		
油豆腐 ---------------------- 3 塊			

1　┌ 鹽 ----------------- 1 ¼小匙
　　├ 胡椒粉 ------------- ½小匙
　　└ 味精 ----------------- ¼小匙

1 芋頭洗淨切成 1 × 6 公分長條，油豆腐切片狀，鍋熱入油 3 杯燒至 7 分熱（1 6 0 ℃），入芋頭炸至金黃色撈起；另鍋內留油 5 大匙，將蒜末炸至金黃色撈起即為蒜茸酥。

2 高湯煮開，入油豆腐、芋頭、米粉煮開改小火煮 1 0 分鐘，再入 **1** 料續煮 5 分鐘，起鍋前再灑上蒜茸酥即可。

450g.(1lb.) ------ thick rice noodles (wet)	3 ---- deep fried bean curd
400g.(14oz.) ---- taros (net weight)	2T. ----------- minced garlic
	12C. ------------------- stock

1　┌ • 1 ¼t.salt
　　└ • ½t.pepper

1 Wash taros, cut into 1 cm x 6 cm (²/₅" x 2½") long strips. Slice bean curd. Heat the wok, add 3C. oil and heat to 160°C (320°F), deep fry taros until golden. Keep 5T. oil in the wok and fry garlic until golden. Remove crispy garlic flakes.

2 Bring stock to a boil, add bean curd, taros, and rice noodles. Bring to a boil again, simmer over low heat for 10 minutes. Season with **1**, simmer for 5 minutes. Sprinkle on garlic flakes and serve.

大腸米粉 •*Pork Intestine Soup Rice Noodles*

豬大腸 ----------- 1 5 0 0 公克	油蔥酥 ------------------------- ½ 杯		
粗米粉（乾）------ 3 0 0 公克	芹菜末 -------------------- 6 大匙		

1－
- 蔥段 ------------------- 5 段
- 薑片 -------------------- 3 片
- 酒 -------------------- 2 大匙

2－
- 鹽 ------------------- 1½ 小匙
- 味精、胡椒粉 --- 各 ½ 小匙

1 大腸洗淨川燙備用。另 **1** 料加水煮開後，入大腸煮至大腸熟爛
（約 9 0 分鐘，煮時須不斷加水），取出大腸切 2 公分段。

2 米粉先泡水 5 分鐘備用。

3 取煮大腸之高湯 8 杯，加 **2** 料及米粉煮 1 5 分鐘，再入大腸煮
開，隨即加芹菜末和油蔥酥即可。

1500g.(3³/₁₀lb.) ------- large pork intestines	½C. ---- fried shallot flakes
300g.(10½oz.) ------- thick rice noodles (dried)	6T. ---------- minced celery

1－
- •5 sections green onion
- •3 slices ginger
- •2T.cooking wine

2－
- •1½t.salt
- •½t.pepper

1 Clean and parboil large pork intestines. Bring water and **1** to a boil, add intestines, water must cover intestines. Simmer until tender for about 90 minutes (boiling water should be added, from time to time, to maintain water level). Remove and cut into 2 cm (³/₄") long sections.

2 Soak rice noodles in water for 5 minutes, drain.

3 Bring 8C. intestine soup to a boil, add **2** and rice noodles, simmer for 15 minutes. Add intestines and bring to a boil again. Sprinkle on minced celery and shallot flakes. Serve hot.

什錦炒米粉 • *Mixed Fried Rice Noodles*

乾米粉（細） ------ ３００公克　　　高湯 ------------------------- ２杯
瘦肉 ----------------- １２０公克

1
　蝦米 ------------- ２０公克
　香菇 ------------- ８公克
　蔥段 ----------------- １４段
　薑片 ------------------- ６片

2
　胡蘿蔔 -------- １５０公克
　花枝 ----------- １２０公克

3
　洋火腿 ----------- ６０公克
　芹菜 ------------- ５０公克

4
　醬油、太白粉 -- 各１小匙
　酒 --------------------- ½小匙

5
　鹽、味精 --------- 各³⁄₄小匙
　胡椒粉 --------------- ¼小匙

1 米粉泡軟，香菇泡軟去蒂切絲，芹菜去葉切段，胡蘿蔔、花枝、火腿、瘦肉均切絲，瘦肉入 **4** 料醃１０分鐘備用。

2 鍋熱入油２杯燒至五分熱（１２０℃），入肉絲過油撈起，鍋內留油４大匙燒熱，入蝦米、**1** 料爆香，續入 **2** 料炒熟，再入高湯煮開，並加 **5** 料調味後，入米粉拌炒至湯汁收乾，最後再入 **3** 料、肉絲炒拌均勻即可。

300g.(10½oz.) --- thin rice noodles (dried)　　120g.(4¼oz.) --- lean pork
2C. --------------------- stock

1
• 20g.(⅔oz.) dried baby shrimp
• 8g.(¼oz.) dried black mushrooms
• 14 sections green onion
• 6 slices ginger

2
• 150g.(5⅓oz.) carrots
• 120g.(4¼oz.) squids

3
• 60g.(2¹⁄₁₀oz.) ham
• 50g.(1¾oz.) celery

4
• 1t.each soy sauce, corn starch
• ½t.cooking wine

5
• ¾t.salt
• ¼t.pepper

1 Soften rice noodles in water. Soften dried mushrooms in warm water, discard stems and shred. Trim off leaves, and cut celery into serving sections. Shred carrots, squids, ham, and pork. Marinate pork in **4** for 10 minutes.

2 Heat the wok, add 2C. oil and heat to 120°C (248°F). Briefly dip pork in hot oil and remove. Keep 4T. oil in the wok, stir fry shrimp and **1** until fragrant. Add **2**, stir fry until cooked. Pour in stock and bring to a boil, season with **5**. Add rice noodles, stir constantly until stock is reduced. Then mix in **3** and pork, mix well and heat thoroughly. Serve.

綠豆糕 •*Green Bean Cake*

奶油 ----------------- １００公克	豆沙 -------------------- ７５公克

❶－⌈ 綠豆粉 -------- １５０公克
　　　熟糯米粉 -------- ５０公克
　　　糖粉 ---------------------½杯

1 將❶料均勻過篩為糕粉，豆沙分成１５等份備用。
2 將奶油溶化拌入糕粉內拌勻分成３０等份，取２份糕粉夾入１份豆沙餡，壓入模型中成型後扣出，再入已墊上乾紗布的蒸籠內以大火蒸１分鐘即可。

100g.(3½oz.) ---- butter or margarine
75g.(2⅔oz.) ----- red bean paste

❶－⌈ •150g.(5⅓oz.) mung bean powder
　　　•50g.(1¾oz.) roasted glutinous rice flour
　　　•½C.powdered sugar

1 Mix **❶** well and sift, this will be the cake flour. Divide red bean paste into 15 equal portions.
2 Melt butter or margarine, mix well with cake flour, divide into 30 equal portions. Stuff one portion of red bean paste into two portions of rice dough. Press in mold, invert when set. Place into a cloth-lined steamer, steam over high heat for 1 minute.

花生糕 • *Peanut Cake*

奶油 ----------------- 100公克		熟糯米粉 ----- 200公克
模型 ------------------------- 一組	**❶**	糖粉 ----------------------- 3/4杯
		花生粉 ----------------- 1/2杯

1 **❶** 料拌勻過篩,加入溶化的奶油拌勻至無顆粒,即為糕粉。
2 稱25公克糕粉,壓入模型中成形後扣出,再入已墊上乾紗布的蒸籠以大火蒸30秒即可。

100g.(3½oz.) ---- butter or margarine		•200g.(7oz.) roasted glutinous rice flour
1 set ------------------- mold	**❶**	•3/4C.powdered sugar
		•½.peanut powder

1 Mix **❶** well and sift. Add melted butter or margarine, mix well until smooth.
2 Press 25g.(⁸/₉oz.) of dough into a mold, invert when set. Place into a cloth-lined steamer, steam over high heat for 30 seconds.

芝麻糕 • *Sesame Cake*

奶油 ----------------- 115公克		熟糯米粉 ----- 150公克
模型 ------------------------- 一組	**❶**	黑芝麻粉 ----- 115公克
		糖粉 --------------------- 3/4杯

1 **❶** 料拌勻過篩,加入溶化的奶油,拌勻至無顆粒,即為糕粉。
2 稱25公克糕粉,壓入模型中成形後扣出,再入已墊上乾紗布的蒸籠以大火蒸30秒即可。

115g.(4oz.) ------ butter or margarine		•150g.(5⅓oz.) roasted glutinous rice flour
1 set ------------------- mold	**❶**	•115g.(4oz.) black sesame powder
		•3/4C.powderd sugar

1 Mix **❶** well and sift, mix in melted butter or margarine, knead until smooth.
2 Press 25g. dough into a mold, invert when set. Place into a cloth-lined steamer, steam over high heat for 30 seconds.

梅香糕 • *Plum Flavored Cake*

奶油 ----------------- 150公克
模型 ------------------------- 一組
1 ┌ 梅子粉、熟糯米粉 --------
      ├ ---------------- 各200公克
      └ 糖粉 -------------------- 1杯

1 1 料拌勻過篩，加入溶化的奶油，拌勻至無顆粒，即為糕粉。
2 稱30公克糕粉，壓入模型中成形後扣出，再入已墊上乾紗布的蒸籠以大火蒸30秒即可。
■ 梅子粉可以酸梅片或仙楂片磨碎後代替。

150g.(5⅓oz.) ---- butter or margarine
1 set ------------------- mold
1 ┌ •200g.(7oz.)each plum powder, roasted glutinous rice flour
      └ •1C.powdered sugar

1 Mix **1** well and sift, add melted butter or margarine, then mix well until smooth.
2 Press 30g. (1oz.) dough into a mold, invert when set. Place into a cloth-lined steamer, steam over high heat for 30 seconds.
■ Crushed candied sour plum or crushed candied hawthorn may be used instead of plum powder.

杏仁糕 • *Almond Cake*

奶油 ----------------- 150公克
模型 ------------------------- 一組
1 ┌ 杏仁霜、熟糯米粉 --------
      ├ ---------------- 各150公克
      └ 糖粉 ----------------- 5大匙

1 1 料拌勻過篩，加入溶化的奶油拌勻至無顆粒，即為糕粉。
2 稱25公克的糕粉，壓入模型中成形後扣出，再入已墊上乾紗布的蒸籠內以大火蒸30秒即可。

150g.(5⅓oz.) ---- butter or margarine
1 set ------------------- mold
1 ┌ •150g.(5⅓oz.)each roasted glutinous rice flour, almond powder
      └ •5T.powdered sugar

1 Mix **1** well and sift. Add melted butter or margarine, mix well until smooth.
2 Press 25g. (⁸⁄₉oz.) of dough into a mold, invert when set. Place into a cloth-lined steamer, steam over high heat for 30 seconds.

鳳片糕 • *Quick Method Dessert*

熟糯米粉 ----------- 600公克	香蕉油 --------------------- ¼小匙	600g.(1⅓lb.) ------ roasted glutinous rice flour	¼t. -------- banana essence
豆沙 ---------------- 450公克	太白粉、食用紅色6號 各少許	450g.(1lb.)red bean paste	dash ------ corn starch, red food coloring

1[細糖 ------------------- 4杯
　開水 ----------------- 1¾杯

1 料加熱至糖溶化，待涼備用。

2 熟糯米粉入❶料及香蕉油拌勻成粉漿狀，不加蓋放置10分鐘，粉漿會稍為變硬，再以手拌揉（圖1）至軟硬適中，（若會黏手，可在手上沾少許太白粉），即為粉糰。

3 粉糰切成每個200公克，包入豆沙50公克（圖2），外沾少許熟糯米粉，入模型中壓平成形（圖3），扣出刷上色素即可。

1[•4C.sugar
　•1¾C.water

1 Heat ❶ until sugar is dissolved, allow to cool.

2 Mix rice flour with ❶ and banana essence, knead well (illus. 1) until medium soft (dust some corn starch if it sticks to fingers).

3 Cut the dough into 200g.(7oz.) pieces, and wrap dough around a 50g.(1¾oz,) piece of red bean paste filling (illus. 2), dust with some rice flour. Press into the mold (illus. 3). Invert and brush on coloring. Any mold and color may be used, depending on personal taste.

1

2

3

鹹酥糕 • *Shallot Cake*

熟糯米粉 ----------- 188公克	糖粉 -------------------------¾杯	188g.(6²/₃oz.) ----- roasted glutinous rice flour	60g.(2¹/₁₀oz.) -- red shallots
奶油 ----------------- 112公克	白芝麻 -------------------- 3大匙	112g.(4oz.) ------ butter or margarine	¾C. ------ powdered sugar
紅蔥頭 ---------------- 60公克	鹽 -------------------------⅛小匙		3T. --- white sesame seeds
			⅛t. ----------------------- salt

1 白芝麻入鍋炒至金黃色，紅蔥頭切片備用。

2 鍋熱入油1杯燒至四分熱（100℃），入紅蔥頭小火炸至金黃色撈起，瀝油備用。

3 白芝麻、紅蔥頭用擀麵棍壓碎並與鹽混合均勻，即為油蔥餡。

4 奶油溶化後與糯米粉、糖粉拌勻，再入油蔥餡拌勻後，稱25公克壓入模型中（圖1），成形後扣出，再放置在墊有乾紗布之蒸籠內（圖2），入鍋大火蒸40秒即可。

1 Roast sesame seeds in a dry pan until golden. Slice shallots.

2 Heat the wok, add 1C. oil and heat to 100℃ (212℉), deep fry shallots over low heat until golden, lift out and drain.

3 Crush sesame seeds and fried shallot flakes with a rolling pin, mix with salt for the shallot filling.

4 Melt butter or margarine, mix well with rice flour, sugar and shallot filling. Press 25g.(⁸/₉oz.) of mixture into the mold (illus. 1). Invert into a cheese cloth-lined steamer (illus. 2). Steam over high heat for 40 seconds.

1

2

味全家政班

味全家政班創立於民國五十年,經過三十餘年的努力,它不只是國內歷史最悠久的家政研習班,更成為一所正式學制之外的專門學校。

創立之初,味全家政班以教授中國菜及研習烹飪技術為主,因教學成果良好,備受各界讚譽,乃於民國五十二年,增闢插花、工藝、美容等各門專科,精湛的師資,教學內容的充實,深獲海內外的肯定與好評。

三十餘年來,先後來班參與研習的學員已近二十萬人次,學員的足跡遍及台灣以外,更有許多國外的團體或個人專程抵台,到味全家政班求教,在習得中國菜烹調的精髓後,或返回居住地經營餐飲業,或擔任家政教師,或獲聘為中國餐廳主廚者大有人在,成就倍受激賞。

近年來,味全家政班亟力研究開發改良中國菜餚,並深入國際間,採集各種精緻、道地美食,除了樹立中華文化「食的精神」外,並將各國烹飪口味去蕪存菁,擷取地方特色。為了確保這些研究工作更加落實,我們特將這些集合海內外餐飲界與研發單位的精典之作,以縝密的拍攝技巧與專業編輯,出版各式食譜,以做傳承。

薪傳與發揚中國烹飪的藝術,是味全家政班一貫的理念,日後,也將秉持宗旨,永續不輟。

Wei-Chuan
Cooking School

Since its establishment in 1961, Wei-Chuan Cooki School has made a continuous commitment towa improving and modernizing the culinary art of cooki and special skills training. As a result, it is the olde and most successful school of its kind in Taiwan.

In the beginning, Wei-Chuan Cooking School w primarily teaching and researching Chinese cooki techniques. However, due to popular demand, t curriculum was expanded to cover courese in flow arrangements, handcrafts, beauty care, dress maki and many other specialized fields by 1963.

The fact that almost 200,000 students, from Taiwa and other countries all over the world, have matric lated in this school can be directly attributed to the hig quality of the teaching staff and the excellent curric lum provided to the studends. Many of the graduat have become successful restaurant owners and chef and in numerous cases, respected teachers.

While Wei-Chuan Cooking School has always bee committed to developing and improving Chinese c sine, we have recently extended our efforts towa gathering information and researching recipes fro defferent provinces of China. With the same dedic tion to accuracy and perfection as always, we hav begun to publish these authentic regional gourm recipes for our devoted readers. These new public tions will continue to reflect the fine tradition of quali our public has grown to appreciate and expect.

純靑食譜 傳遞溫馨

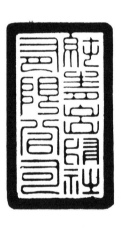

純青食譜　版權所有

局版台業字第3884號
中華民國83年6月初版發行
定價：新台幣貳佰伍拾元整